CAMBRIDGE LIBRARY COLLECTION

Books of enduring scholarly value

Literary Studies

This series provides a high-quality selection of early printings of literary works, textual editions, anthologies and literary criticism which are of lasting scholarly interest. Ranging from Old English to Shakespeare to early twentieth-century work from around the world, these books offer a valuable resource for scholars in reception history, textual editing, and literary studies.

The Times on the American War

The biographer and writer on philosophy, ethics and literature Leslie Stephen (1832–1904) was educated at Eton, King's College, London, and then Trinity College, Cambridge, where he remained as a fellow and a tutor for his entire career. He served as the first editor (1885–91) of the *Dictionary of National Biography* and in 1871 he became editor of the *Cornhill Magazine*. In this short piece, published in 1865, Stephen takes issue with the portrayal of the American Civil War (1861–5) by *The Times*. Having travelled to the United States himself in 1863, Stephen argues that the newspaper's depiction of the events in America is inaccurate, and both misinforms the public in Britain and damages Britain's reputation abroad. Also included in this reissue is a short article on the poet John Byrom (1692–1763), and an obituary of Henry Sidgwick (1838–1900), Stephen's personal friend.

Cambridge University Press has long been a pioneer in the reissuing of out-of-print titles from its own backlist, producing digital reprints of books that are still sought after by scholars and students but could not be reprinted economically using traditional technology. The Cambridge Library Collection extends this activity to a wider range of books which are still of importance to researchers and professionals, either for the source material they contain, or as landmarks in the history of their academic discipline.

Drawing from the world-renowned collections in the Cambridge University Library and other partner libraries, and guided by the advice of experts in each subject area, Cambridge University Press is using state-of-the-art scanning machines in its own Printing House to capture the content of each book selected for inclusion. The files are processed to give a consistently clear, crisp image, and the books finished to the high quality standard for which the Press is recognised around the world. The latest print-on-demand technology ensures that the books will remain available indefinitely, and that orders for single or multiple copies can quickly be supplied.

The Cambridge Library Collection brings back to life books of enduring scholarly value (including out-of-copyright works originally issued by other publishers) across a wide range of disciplines in the humanities and social sciences and in science and technology.

The Times
on the
American War

And Other Essays

Leslie Stephen

CAMBRIDGE
UNIVERSITY PRESS

CAMBRIDGE UNIVERSITY PRESS

Cambridge, New York, Melbourne, Madrid, Cape Town,
Singapore, São Paolo, Delhi, Mexico City

Published in the United States of America by Cambridge University Press, New York

www.cambridge.org
Information on this title: www.cambridge.org/9781108047623

© in this compilation Cambridge University Press 2012

This edition first published 1865–1900
This digitally printed version 2012

ISBN 978-1-108-04762-3 Paperback

THE "TIMES"

ON THE

AMERICAN WAR:

A HISTORICAL STUDY.

BY L. S.

LONDON:

WILLIAM RIDGWAY, 169, PICCADILLY, W.

MDCCCLXV.

———

Price One Shilling and Sixpence.

LONDON :
PRINTED BY JAS. WADE,
18, TAVISTOCK STREET, COVENT GARDEN

THE "TIMES"

AMERICAN WAR.

I.—THE " TIMES " ON AMERICAN AFFAIRS.

IN discussing the causes of the Crimean war, Mr. Kinglake gives a prominent place to the agency of the *Times*. He does not decide whether the *Times* was the master or the slave of the British people, whether it prompted their decisions, or merely divined them by a happy instinct. The coincidence of sentiment between the *Times* and common sentiment is explicable on either hypothesis. A story, however, is related by Mr. Kinglake, which, if it is to be accepted as authentic, would tend to clear up the mystery. The *Times*, he says, used to employ a shrewd, idle clergyman, whose duty was to hang about in places of public resort, to listen neither to the pre-eminently foolish nor to the pre-eminently wise, but to wait till some common and obvious thought was repeated in many places by many average men all unacquainted with each other. That thought was the prize he sought for, and brought home to his employers. Once in possession of this knowledge, they again employed able writers to enforce this opinion by arguments certain to fall upon willing ears. The *Times* was meanwhile regarded by ordinary men and women as a mysterious entity, a concrete embodiment of the power known in the abstract as " public opinion." As Mr. Kinglake says, men prefixed to its name such adjectives as

showed "that they regarded the subject of their comments in the
" light of an active sentient being, having a life beyond the span
" of mortal men, gifted with reason, armed with a cruel strength,
" endued with some of the darkest of human passions, but clearly
" liable hereafter to the direst penalty of sin." They supposed it,
I may add, to be in possession of a political knowledge pro-
founder than the knowledge of any private individual, if not than
the knowledge of statesmen, and acquiesced in its arrogating the
right of speaking in the name of the English people.

It is, however, notorious that no part of the power wielded by
the *Times* is derived from any respect for its consistency or its
unselfish advocacy of principles. And this follows naturally if we
accept as substantially accurate the account given by Mr. Kinglake
of the process by which its opinions are determined. A thought
common to the great mass of the educated English classes must
in all cases be a tolerably obvious one : if it refers to domestic
matters which are familiar in all their bearings to the majority
of educated men, it will probably be marked by shrewd common-
sense ; when thousands of Englishmen agree in thinking that
the suffrage is unfairly distributed, or that trade is oppressively
taxed, they are probably right. Their opinions are, at least,
the result of an operation which may, without a palpable
misnomer, be described as thought. In such cases, the *Times*,
in concentrating their opinions into one focus, will adopt a
policy which, if not resting upon very exalted considerations, is
at least dictated by homely good sense, and not marked by utter
ignorance. But the case is widely different when we come to
foreign politics. English ignorance in such matters is proverbial.
The name of America five years ago called up to the ordinary
English mind nothing but a vague cluster of associations, com-
pounded of Mrs. Trollope, *Martin Chuzzlewit*, and *Uncle
Tom's Cabin*. A few flying reminiscences of disputes about
territory, and a few commonplaces about democracy, made up

what we were pleased to call our opinions. Most people were as ignorant of American history since the revolution as of the history of the Chinese empire, and of American geography as of the geography of Central Africa. Our utterances on American affairs might have the external form of judgment; they were, in substance, mere random assertions about unknown quantities. Now, the *Times*, by the law of its being, would have to be the mere echo of these sham decisions. The honest British public confidently laid down the law, like a Dogberry giving judgment in a Chancery suit, and the *Times* stood by as a skilful reporter to dress its blundering dogmas in the language of political philosophy. The British public talked about " Yankee snobbishness;" the *Times* translated its words into solemn nothings about " American democracy," and the public thought it had said rather a good thing.

I wish to trace some of the consequences of this peculiar process, by which a newspaper transmutes our rubbish into a kind of Britannia metal, and obtains our sympathy because we have ourselves provided the raw material, and our admiration because it is worked up into such sparkling tinsel. The very first necessity for this dexterous shuffling is an affectation of absolute infallibility; a true account of the *Times* would run like Prince Henry's description of Poins, " Thou art a blessed fellow to think " as every man thinks, never a man's thought in the world keeps " the roadway better than thine." But it would never suit our modern Poins to be praised for merely keeping the roadway; he must be credited with also pointing it out; and, to substantiate his claims of guiding the English people instead of merely divining the path which they will take, he must naturally affect more than mortal wisdom. His claim to be followed is that he is always right. And the *a posteriori* proof that the *Times* has been right harmonizes beautifully with this *a priori* claim to confidence. Everybody, it says, agrees with us; therefore we are right; everybody always has agreed with us, therefore we have been always right. The *Times*, like the figure-head of a ship, always leads public opinion; and, as we have always been following it, it must have been going in the same direction. The beauty of this is that the *Times* in arrogating infallibility and consistency contrives to insinuate delicate flattery to its constituents. No one can deny a claim to consistency founded upon perfect agreement with his own past opinions.

So far, then, the *Times* is only to be accused of passing off false gems for true, affecting all the time to be a profound and an honest connoisseur. But a little reflection will show, what this pamphlet is intended to illustrate by a striking example—namely, the danger to which this course exposes us. In our ignorance of the cause of some great foreign convulsion, we judge of it partly by the way in which it affects our interests, and partly in accord-ance with certain traditional prejudices. There must be some-thing radically wrong in a war which affects our supplies of cotton ; and we cannot credit a race who chew tobacco and wear bowie knives with any heroic virtues. Judgments really deter-mined by shallow prejudices can only be supported by constant perversion of the facts. Ignorant people, even though they affect to be infallible, can pervert facts with genuine unconsciousness. They deduce their premises from their conclusions without the least guess that they are illogical. It is only necessary to fix the attention upon the set of facts that make for the side they have taken, and to shut their eyes to all others. Thus the next step of our infallible expounder of national opinions is to lay down authoritatively a theory, intended not so much to be accurate, as to serve as some justification for that which has come by a kind of accident to be the popular opinion. The evil which follows from this is obvious. The American naturally believes that the *Times* is, in fact, the authorized mouthpiece of English sentiment. He credits it with all the mysterious knowledge which it claims to possess, and assumes that in listening to it he hears the matured opinions of the most educated and reflective minds of England. Finding a complete perversion of his case, he naturally again attributes it to malice rather than ignorance. He cannot believe that such pretended wisdom covers so much emptiness ; and he attributes to wilful falsehood what is at worst a desire to flatter its readers, overriding a love of severe historical truth. Our American thus assumes very falsely, though very naturally, that the English people hate him, abuse him, refuse to see his merits, and knowingly accept the vilest caricatures of his purpose ; he does not understand that we have stumbled into mistakes, and that our blunders have been pampered and exaggerated by our flatterers. He would naturally reply by abuse to our abuse ; even if his own press had not already acted with as much recklessness and want of principle as the *Times*. And so the good feeling, for which should all wish, is hopelessly destroyed for a time.

In explaining the process more in detail, I hope I may render some slight service towards producing a better understanding. I cannot see the force of a late piteous appeal of the *Times* "to let bygones be bygones." It is sufficiently impudent after abusing a man incessantly, and being mistaken in all you have said, to request him to forget all about it. " I have been spitting upon " your Jewish gaberdine, calling you misbeliever, cutthroat dog, " and other pretty names for four years; but now—I freely forgive " you."

This, however, I leave the *Times* to reconcile with its own lofty sense of dignity. I wish bygones to be bygones, as between the English and American peoples, for I think that each has misunderstood the other. The most effective way of securing this result would be to throw our Jonahs overboard, to upset the credit of the mischief-makers who have interfered between us, and to withdraw our countenance from the blustering impostor who has been speaking all this time in our name without any due authority. Two men sometimes quarrel because each has been barked at by his neighbour's cur, and fancies that his neighbour has set it on. The best way of making peace is to prove that, after all, it is nothing but a dog barking.

II.—The "Times" as a Prophet.

If a man may be pardoned for prophesying at all in political matters, he may be pardoned for making frequent blunders. No human intelligence can unravel the complicated play of forces by which the fate of nations is determined ; and yet much may be learned from a man's prophecies. They show us by implication what view he takes of the present, though they may throw very little light on the future. If a man should tell us that Heenan was certain to beat Sayers because he had drawn first blood, we should set him down as a bad judge of prize-fighting. His prophecy would prove him ignorant of the very conditions of the noble art, or ignorant of the strength of Sayers' constitution. By quoting a few prophecies from the *Times*, it will, I think, be tolerably evident that it had completely omitted from its calculations some element which ought to have been taken into account. There is one other point to be noticed. The *Times* may reply to some of its adversaries—We both prophesied in the dark, and though your prophecy came right and mine wrong, that is nothing to boast of. This excuse will hardly serve to account for the fact that the *Times* has prophesied the success of the South as confidently as the success of the North, and for the further fact that it has always boasted of its consistency and foresight. I will quote a few of its vaticinations.

Nov. 26, 1860.—" It is evident, on the smallest reflection, that " the South, even if united, could never resist for three months " the greatly preponderating strength of the North."

April 30, 1861.—It hopes that "the certain failure of all

" attempts at coercion will be discovered by the Washington
" Government soon enough to save the country from being
" drenched in blood."

May 9, 1861.—" The reduction of the seceding States is an
" almost inconceivable idea."

July 18.—" No war of independence ever terminated unsuc-
" cessfully except where the disparity of force is far greater
" than it is in this case," and (July 19) " We prefer a frank recog-
" nition of Southern independence to the policy avowed in
" the President's message, solely because we foresee, as by-
" standers, that this is the issue in which, after infinite loss and
" humiliation, the contest must result."

The character thus indicated of the philosophic bystander
seeing things more clearly than was given to the foolish and pig-
headed Northerners who persisted in going their own way, was
perhaps that in which the *Times* most delighted to appear.

Aug. 27.—It appears in the same character, modified by a
stronger dash of the profound philosopher. England, it says,
might as well attempt to conquer France, or, indeed, better; for
the Northerners are not (as we should, of course, be in the case
supposed) agreed amongst themselves. The only parallel in
history is the French invasion of Russia, but Napoleon had far
greater resources than the North, and the South is far stronger
than Russia. " We are in a condition to give advice," which is,
in short, for North and South to part friends. The *Times* never
could learn, though incessantly burning its fingers, to keep clear
of these dangerous historical parallels.

By the beginning of 1862 it had become still more confident.
January 14, 1862, it declares that this was a case " in which
" success was only possible with overwhelming odds ; but here
" the odds were all on the Southern side." As throwing some
light upon this audacious assertion, I may quote the *Times* of
September 24, 1862, where, in anticipation of Maryland rising to

join Lee, it says, that the South have at this moment more than half the total population on their side; and it makes a rough calculation, apparently in utter ignorance of the census, and certainly in the flattest contradiction to it, of the rival forces. There were, it says, twelve millions on the side of the North, nine on the side of the South, and eight millions "between," who are now gravitating to the Southern side. Now, as in all the Slave States, including the Border States, which never left the Union, there are only just twelve millions, and as there are nineteen millions of distinct Northern population, the *Times* has here been cooking its facts in a manner quite beyond my powers of arithmetic. On April 30 it had spoken of a "dozen great "territories, with eight million inhabitants, as warlike as any on "the face of the globe." September 30, it proved that the blockade must be ineffective and could only slightly raise the price of cotton. "If the war were only safe to last, we can imagine "no surer way of making a fortune than by setting about to "baffle its Custom-house officers and cruisers,"—a silly remark enough, because the chance of making a fortune necessarily implies a great risk, but illustrative of the predictive powers of the *Times*. Six months afterwards (March 8, 1862) it was engaged in proving that the blockade was already effective.

Jan. 15, 1862.—The *Times*, perhaps, culminated as a prophet. "How long," it inquired, "is this to last? Not long enough "for the conquest of the South. Shall we give the volunteers two "months as the period necessary to enlighten them as to the "difference between paper dollars and silver dollars? It will be "ample time. We need not give the contractors nearly so "long. . . . The army of the Potomac will melt away in-"sensibly, or, if it be so unfortunate as to be down South, it will "die away unfed and unsuccoured in the swamps of Secessia. "The beginning of the end has come." The *Times* announced that it was impossible to carry on war (that is, as it explained afterwards, " offensive war") upon paper money ; and a collapse would necessarily follow in two months. Truly, prophets should read history.

A singular thing now happened. The North perversely, and in utter disregard of the *Times*, took New Orleans, Fort Donelson, Newberne, Beaufort, and other places, and seemed to be carrying all before them. The *Times* at once showed, as I shall have hereafter to remark, several signs of conversion to their cause. For the present I need only mention its prophecies.

March 31.—It confesses with interesting frankness that all calculations (all its calculations) had gone wrong " on account " of the unexpected and unastonishing resolution of the North, " of which it would be unjust to depreciate the spirit, &c." We failed to sympathize, " not that we sympathized with slave- " holders or approved the wilful destruction of a great political " fabric, but that we thought the fact accomplished and its " reversal beyond possibility."

The resources of the North have now begun to tell. They are twenty millions to ten, and can command the sea. (On July 21, four months later, they speak contemptuously of " the " few shallow reasoners in this country, who are always telling " us that twenty milllons must in the end beat ten millions"— " a silly fallacy" which had received a practical refutation in M'Clellan's defeat.) The slaves had not risen, as was predicted. As for finances, "it is beyond all question that the North is getting on smoothly enough for the present." Still, if the South persevered, they must establish their independence.

May 28.—" That the Federals have established an ascendency in " the field is beyond all question." " The whole story is a mystery " as well as a marvel. It is almost as hard to believe what has " occurred as to imagine what may ultimately happen." To call a thing a mystery is to make two assertions : one, that you don't understand it yourself ; the other, that no one else understands it.

June 28.—After a long discussion of the war, it comes to the conclusion, "the superior numbers and resources of the North we look upon as certain in the end to prevail."

Directly after so positive an assertion, and shortly after a declaration, that the whole story was "a mystery and a marvel," I am not surprised to find the *Times* recover its complacency at a bound. M'Clellan's expedition was at a standstill.

July 3, 1862.—"We," it says, "have been right, and the North "wrong in so many things that our opinion is at any rate entitled "to consideration." "We" means England, with the exception of an insignificant minority, and, of course, as interpreted by the *Times*.

And for the next two years and a half, it prophesies with unabated vigour in the old direction. The only pause was during the spring of 1864, and is to be attributed probably to the Schleswig-Holstein difficulties which attracted the public attention.

I will give a few specimens, though many are unnecessary, as models of pointed, vigorous, and unfulfilled prediction.

Sept. 11.—The talk of putting down the rebellion, punishing treason, "putting down and crushing out rebellion, is mere verbiage."

Jan. 17, 1863 (in answer to Mr. Bright).—"We have committed "the unpardonable crime of giving the Government of the "Northern States credit for some good sense and humanity. We "have predicted that sooner or later the North must see that its "enterprise is hopeless, and that it must submit, as the mother "country submitted eighty years ago. We have been mistaken "thus far, not in the fortunes of war, not in our calculation of the "Confederate strength or weakness, not in the cost of the war or "the condition of American finance, but in the one single hope that "the Federals would see what all the world except themselves see."

March 19.—" They might as well try to save it (the Union) as "the Heptarchy."

The next is a very pretty specimen of the genuine *Times* mixtures ; a little fine writing, a good deal of arrogance, and a spice of unmixed abuse all delivered from the " philosophical bystander" point of view.

May 28.—People "naturally asked whether the gentleman " was to rule in the old world and the opposite character in " the new. It is vain to look for those higher principles from " which alone we might expect any settlement of the question. " . . . If they persist in the rule of might, there is only " one result, they will just annihilate one another. A miserable " remnant, a ruined country, a relapse into savagery, and other " evils unknown and inconceivable will be the only possible " result. . . . From this vantage ground" (that of the British Constitution) " we tell these poor drowning wretches that they " have no chance whatever, but to forget their dream of infinite " numbers, of boundless territory, of inexhaustible wealth, and " irresistible might, and bow low like children to the teaching of " right. Let them just consider what they ought to do, and what " ' ought' means, and have some chance of getting out of this " difficulty without blasting a whole continent. We do not say " this is an easy or altogether a pleasant course, but it is the " only course that does not lead to utter destruction."

The poor wretches would not drown, but the *Times* was not disheartened.

July 21.—"We forecast very naturally and pleasantly that as " reunion is impossible, and the only object of fighting is to have " the last blow, the winning side would be glad to make a kind " and generous use of its advantage."

Aug. 31.—We find the philosophic bystander again. " In every " civil war the combatants have been blind to prospects that every " bystander could foresee ; and we suppose this terrible and cruel " struggle will linger on till the North has no means left to fight, " and the South nothing but freedom left to fight for."

Oct. 19.—We come across a new and ingeniously accurate historical parallel. "It will be found as impossible to overwhelm " the native levies of men of English race fighting for their lives " and possessions" (a delicate periphrasis for slaves) "by any " number of foreign hirelings as it was for Carthage with the " greatest general the world ever saw at the head of her armies, " and the wealth of the world at her command, to hire Gauls, " Spaniards, and Numidians enough to break down the stubborn " spirit of the less ably led Roman militia. A nation fighting for " its liberty may not come victorious out of the conflict, but " history affords no example that we are aware of, of an invasion " and subjection of a warlike people by an invader who scarcely " ever was enabled to sleep on the field of battle and whose con- " stant boast was not that he had routed his enemy, but that he " placed his army in safety."

Dec. 24.—"Yet, though we greatly underrated" (as is now evident) " the difficulties of the North, the opinion was almost " universal that subjugation of the South was impossible. Even " when the North has surrendered her liberty and beggared her " finances, she will not be able permanently to hold these immense " countries and keep down their hostile populations on these terms."

In the early part of 1864 prophecies became rare, as I have already remarked. Although the *Times* vehemently denied any value to the Northern successes, it probably felt that the taking of Vicksburg and the battle of Gettysburg had changed the aspect of the war.

Its spirits, however, gradually recovered, and it asserts—

May 3.—"The present prospects of the Confederates in this fourth year of the war are brighter than ever before."

July 5.—The failure of George III. was not more complete " than that which the contemplation of affairs in the middle of " 1864 shows us to have attended the efforts of the Federal " Government."

The next is a specimen of a pleasant figure of speech by which the *Times* occasionally describes itself as " all Europe " :—

Aug. 22.—" The North must see that it is persisting in an " enterprise allowed by all Europe to be hopeless, and proved to " be so by events up to the present time. . . . In Europe " we can only employ the lessons of this unnatural conflict to " confirm our convictions of the hopelessness of the war and " the necessity of a speedy peace."

Sept. 14.—" The public will admit. that they have not been " misguided by our comments. The great fact which we asserted " from the first is now " (six months before the end of the war) " placed beyond the reach of controversy. We said that the " North could never subdue the South, and the North has now " proclaimed the same conclusion." (This refers to the Chicago Convention.)

Oct. 10.—" Ruin stares the Union in the face if the war is to " be conducted by General M'Clellan, and if it be conducted " by President Lincoln the result must be precisely the same."

Nov. 12.—The *Times* made an unintentionally good hit. " The subjugation of the Confederacy must be deferred by the " most sanguine Republican to the spring of 1865."

Dec. 14.—" To negotiation it must come at last, and the " sooner the inevitable resolution is taken the better it will " be for America and the world. . . . We, the bystanders, " saw things more clearly than the actors, and we see them " more clearly now."

Feb. 22, 1865.—After explaining that Americans suffer from a certain " monomania " of devotion to the Union, it adds :— " So long as that idol stands on its pedestal the war must rage " on, and we see no prospect of its early termination."

The *Times* was evidently not quite confident, however, and it endeavoured to effect a strategic movement, of which the nature will appear from the following extracts :—

March 6.—Sherman's "unexampled successes" expose him
to a serious embarrassment. " He takes these towns one after
" another, but they are no use to him when taken.   He is
" experiencing a difficulty which was always foretold.   The
" Federals have regained their military reputation ; but, if the
" South shall resolve to stand out to the end, they have made
" but little progress towards the conclusion of the war."

Its spirits gave way for a moment, and it confesses, March 8;
" The   end   is   not   far :   the   cause   is   simply   bleeding   to
" death."

Once more it rallied.

March 14.—" Everybody   in   Europe "   (I   have   already   explained that this is a circuitous formula for " we " in the *Times*)
" thought   that   the   military   ascendency   which   Sherman   has   at
" length   established   would   have   been   secured   by   the   North   in
" a   single   campaign ;   but   what,   it   was   asked,   would   be   done
" then ?   and   that   is   the   question   before   us   now."   Or,   as   it
says more fully in answer to a speech of Mr. Bright's,—

March 15.—" We   thought   that   the   North   would   instantly
" overrun   the   South,   &c.   &c.   These   things   are   only   now
" beginning to come to pass.   They have come to pass much later
" and   in   a   much   less   degree   than   we   had   anticipated ;   but   then
" we thought, and still think, that the real danger and difficulties
" of   the   conflict   would   begin.   .   .   .   It   remains   to   be   seen
" whether   we   are   wrong   in   these   anticipations.   When   we   are
" shown   to   be   so,   it   will   be   time   to   taunt   us   with   our   mistakes "
(though   it   thinks   Mr.   Bright   has   made   too   many   to   throw   the
first   stone).   " At   any   rate,   we   are   not   yet   convinced   of   our
" error,   and   need   something   more   than   Mr.   Bright's   oracular
" assertion to prove it."

Mr.   Bright   has   quite   a   peculiar   talent   for   striking   flashes   of
nonsense out of the *Times*.

My concluding passage is not exactly a prophecy.

April 19.—" The catastrophe seems complete, and in all its
" accessories calculated to impress people with a feeling that
" the work is accomplished, and that the civil war is really at
" an end."

I lay little stress upon the fact, taken by itself, that the *Times*
prophecies came absurdly wrong. But I say that its errors
were of a class which, besides the ordinary measure of human
fallibility, implies a total misconception of the conditions of
the struggle. An astronomer's prediction of an eclipse might
fail from a mere arithmetical blunder ; or it might fail because
his calculation assumed a wrong configuration of the solar
system. Thus the *Times* believed, or at least it occasionally
asserted, that the South had actually greater resources than the
North. It maintained that the North could not continue the war
for two months, on account of financial exhaustion. In other
words, it was as ignorant of statistics as of history. It failed to
recognize the extraordinary resources of the North, or to
remember that wars can be carried on with a depreciated
currency. It is true that it contradicted itself flatly on both
these points. The superior numbers and resources of the North
were, as it said (June 28, 1862), certain to prevail ; and as it
kindly observed (August 15, 1862), " it is a mistake to suppose that
" money or credit, or tolerable supplies of food, clothing, and
" ordinary comforts are necessary to the work of cutting throats,
" blowing up trains, and burning houses ; " in other words, it was
driven to a paroxysm of abuse, by discovering that the Northern
credit had not collapsed nor the war ceased on account of a suspension of cash payments. But the incessant predictions which
I have quoted are doubtless founded upon the assumptions of
Northern weakness in resources and in credit, and they, therefore,
imply an error, not merely in calculation, but in knowledge of
the primary data.

The great mass of prophetic matter in the *Times* thus implied a false conception of the facts. But it was incapable of even holding steadily to one conception. Before the war began, and in the spring of 1862, its prophecies were diametrically opposite to its prophecies at most other periods. In the spring of 1864 it was neutral. The *Times*, in 1860, anticipated Mr. Seward's prophecy that the North would conquer the South in ninety days. In 1861 it prophesied that the North would abandon its attempts in sixty days. And (November 4, 1862) it endorsed Mr. Jefferson Davis's assertion that the war could be carried on in Virginia for twenty years after the capture of Richmond. Mr. Seward was wrong, and Mr. Davis was wrong; the *Times* had the curious felicity of combining both blunders.

The explanation of this doubtless is, that the *Times* had no fixed theory whatever. It looked on like an ignorant person at a game of whist, knowing nothing of the hands, and therefore crying out as each side took a trick or played a trump that it was certain to win the rubber. It would not believe that, in order to hold its own, the weaker side had played out all its strength, while the stronger had still its best cards in reserve. And thus, while the South was sinking in the final struggle, the *Times* became more confident than ever. Whilst Grant held Lee within the lines of Richmond and Sherman pierced the heart of Georgia, the *Times* was confidently pronouncing the war hopeless, and actually pluming itself in unconscious absurdity upon the confirmation of its sapient predictions. Like a man in a dark room, it knocked its head straight against the wall, without even putting out its hands to save itself.

III.—SLAVERY AND THE WAR.

I have, I hope, raised a *primâ facie* presumption that the *Times* was labouring under some delusion. It had omitted some element from its calculations, sufficient to distort the whole history of the struggle. The story, to use its own words, was "a mystery and a marvel;" it was a mystery and a marvel simply because the *Times* was not in possession of the one clue which led through the labyrinth. A foreigner looking on at a cricket-match is apt to think the evolutions of the players mysterious; and they will be enveloped in sevenfold mystery if he has a firmly preconceived prejudice that the ball has nothing whatever to do with the game. At every new movement, he must invent a new theory to show that the apparent eagerness to pick up the ball is a mere pretext; that no one really wants to hit it, or to catch it, or to throw it at the wickets; and that its constant appearance is due to a mere accident. He will be very lucky if some of his theories do not upset each other.

As, in my opinion, the root of all the errors of the *Times* may be found in its views about slavery, which lay, as is now evident, at the bottom of the whole quarrel, I may be pardoned for recalling very shortly some well-known and now generally recognized truths. I shall then be able to show how the *Times* treated them, and how, by cutting out the central knot of the difficulty, the whole skein fell into hopeless entanglement.

All candid men will admit that the cause of the American war lay in the questions relating to slavery. So many other issues were raised beyond the simple one of abolition or non-abolition, and so many political principles were inextricably interwoven with the question of how to deal with slavery, that interested persons were enabled for a time to impose upon ignorant and superficial observers. Those who judged merely from the confused cries that rose at every moment from the battle-field, instead of inquiring into the antecedents of the conflicting parties, might be easily deceived.

That slavery was in some sense the cause of the war rests upon evidence equal to that which would satisfy the rigid requirements of physical philosophy.   By a simple inspection of the map, it appears that the great rent which divided the Union coincided with the line between slaveholders and non-slaveholders, and coincided with no other line of division.   It divided States, it split masses homogeneous in their agricultural or their commercial interests, but throughout its whole length it divided slavery from free labour.

More than this, the repulsion between the opposing masses varied in direct proportion to the degree in which one was, and the other was not, infected with slavery.   The centres of the slaveholding interest were the centres of secession.   The districts where slavery was dying out were divided in their allegiance. Those where it was legally or practically extinct were unanimous for the Union.

More than this, again, the conflict of interest had led to discussions prolonged over a generation.   More eager and vigorous debates had never raged upon any subject.

Those debates had turned exclusively upon the compromises which might reconcile the rival interests of slaveholders and free men.   From Jefferson to Clay every American statesman had pointed to slavery as the rock upon which the Union was pre-destined to split.   Every compromise that had been devised to reconcile the two sections turned upon slavery, and slavery exclusively.   The Missouri compromise, the compromises of 1850, the compromises that were elaborately discussed at the instance of the Border States on the eve of secession, and with a view to avoiding it, all bore upon slavery, and upon nothing else. To put all this out of sight required stupendous ignorance, or equally stupendous impudence. There was, however, one chance of confusing the question. The Abolitionists in the North held slavery to be an accursed thing, to be attacked at the sacrifice of the Union, or of any merely human institution. The Democrats held that New York could no more interfere with slavery in South Carolina than with slavery in Brazil. The Republicans differed from both parties by holding that the powers of the Constitution enabled them to exclude slavery from the territories, and wished to use those powers so as incidentally to hamper and confine it within fixed limits. The Abolitionists and Republicans held slavery to be pernicious. The Democrats might or might not agree with them. The point upon which they necessarily differed was the right of the free section of the Union to attack slavery directly or indirectly : upon this question there might be any number of shades of opinion. Now it was possible to confound an unwillingness to attack slavery by unconstitutional means with an unwillingness to attack it at all, and thus with indifference to it, or even direct approval of it.

All Englishmen, except habitual drunkards, object to intoxication. None but a small clique would legislate directly against drunkards. It would be as unfair to accuse the *Times* of indifference to the evils of drink, because it respected individual liberty too much to legislate against drinking, as it was to accuse Democrats of necessarily sympathizing with slavery, because they respected State rights too much to attack it even indirectly. But it would be still more unfair to accuse a man of favouring drunkenness who should be in favour of limiting the spread of new public-houses whilst refusing to interfere with the old ; and, in the parallel case, a sincere Republican could, by no honest man, be accused of indifference to slavery. We shall presently see that the *Times* made use of this contemptible sophistry to throw doubt upon the sincerity of the great mass of American parties. To complete the circle of abuse, it was only necessary to accuse the Abolitionists of fanaticism.   A man who denounced slavery at all hazards was called an " exterminater " (their claim to this title has received a curious comment in the fact that the Abolitionists were amongst the most conspicuous advocates of mercy to Jefferson Davis) ; a man who opposed it indirectly, or not at all, was a hypocrite for preferring any other consideration to that of abolition.

And here I may add, that a further amount of doubt was thrown upon the motives of the Northern States by the fact that the chief motive of the great mass was not hatred to slavery, but love of the Union.   No one can doubt that this was the case. Slavery was attacked, not as an evil in itself, but as the cause of evil to the Union ; this is true, but it is a very bad reason for imputing insincerity to the assailants.   I forbid my neighbour to get drunk, not primarily for his good, but because I am afraid that when he gets drunk he will break my head.   This seems to be a very sensible motive.   I am not arguing that Englishmen ought to sympathize with this worship of the Union ; I am only saying that it was grossly unfair to cry out against the sincerity of anti-slavery zeal, because it was in most men's minds the result, and not the cause, of zeal for the Union.

Of the attempt to set up the tariff question as the real point at issue I need say little.   That lie is dead.   It is enough to remark that the tariff which favoured New England manufacturers of Pennsylvanian ironmasters, bore as hardly upon the West as it did upon the South, and still more certainly bore as hardly upon the parts of Virginia and Tennessee which adhered to the Union, as upon the parts which seceded.   The line of separation everywhere followed the tortuous geographical line between slavery and free soil, whilst it cut at right angles the lines bounding opposite commercial interests.   The burden, borne for the benefit of the East, weighed equally upon the West and South ; as it caused no complaints except in the South, we may presume that there discontent was due to some deeper lying influence.

I have endeavoured to lay down this sketch-map the better to exhibit the eccentricity of the course steered by the *Times*. Those who may differ from me as to the relations of some of the principles noticed, may still agree in appreciating the facility with which the *Times* can take them up or lay them down in every possible permutation and combination.

IV.—CHANGE OF THE "TIMES" POLICY.

On the 4th of January, 1861, a letter upon the origin of the war appeared in the *Times*. The conclusions of the writer were summed up in these words, "Whether two systems of labour, one " so dead, the other so full of life, can continue to live side by " side is a problem which the United States are now attempting " to solve for themselves." A historical sketch was given to prove that all political struggles in the States had hitherto turned upon the same question. The *Times*, accepting these conclusions, argued that Mr. Buchanan, the then President, put the question upon too low a ground. Mr. Buchanan, it says, assumed that slavery was indifferent, that New England had no right to discuss it. He never remarks, as it indignantly declares, that " what the Free States " require, they are morally justified in requiring, whilst what the " slave States demand, they can demand only at the cost of " justice and right." If the Union gave no right to discuss slavery, the Union would be so " unsubstantial and shadowy that it ought to be dissolved." But, of course, we " dispute the fact." The South was more responsible than the North for the previous agitation. " We cannot disguise from ourselves that " there is a right and a wrong in this question, and that the right " belongs, with all its advantages, to the States of the North."

During January and February, 1861, the *Times* stopped every logical avenue of escape for Southern advocates. It proved the South to be morally wrong. To put forward such claims necessarily implied a low moral standard. " The North," says the *Times* (January 7, 1861) "are for freedom of discussion. " The South resist freedom of discussion with the tar brush and " the pine fagot." The open avowal of such gross injustice could be accounted for only by the grossest ignorance. It was a kind of madness marvellous in a land of schools and newspapers ; but " the mass of the people of the Southern States are in a state of deplorable ignorance," scarcely better than that of the Irish peasantry. The South Carolina manifesto was (January 19, 1861) remarkable for " utter falsehood." It proved that the State " was " treading the path which leads to the downfall of nations and " the misery of families." But had any one a right to stop them from following that path? The *Times* answered, yes. To the " specious plea" that the South might colonize as well as the North, carrying the peculiar institution with them, " the answer is obvious" (January 28) : Slavery is in very truth a thing " hateful and abominable," and if the South should be so rash as to resist the constraints placed upon it, they would be answerable for the consequences. But the North were justified, not only on grounds of morality, but of expediency. It argues elaborately (January 18) that the North have the strongest reasons for resisting secession. If they gave way, the Union would be broken into fragments, of which all the richest would fall to the South. (March 12.)—If secession were permitted New York would probably set up as a free port. A doubt might still remain as to the constitutionality of Northern interference. Here the *Times* clenches the question by an argument, which would be indeed conclusive, were it not for its betrayal of the flimsy nature of its knowledge. (January 29, 1861.)—In criticizing a speech of Mr. Seward's, it expresses its delight at finding him at last occupying a ground which it is strange that American statesmen should only just have begun to perceive. It illustrates this ground by a pleasant fiction—of a proposal said to have been made some time ago for a simultaneous secession of South Carolina from the United States, and of Lancashire from England, to coalesce into a State based upon cotton and slavery. To such a proceeding we should naturally demur. In the case of Lancashire we should not go back to the agreement between Hugh Lupus and William the Conqueror. South Carolina would of course have no right to go back to the days of Pinckney and Washington. " So far as the Central Government is concerned, there is " absolutely no difference." This is a vigorous statement of the principles of the old Federal party, and of the doctrines which have now been demonstrated at the sword's point. But what follows is an example of an ignorant supporter trumping his partner's best card. The American people, says the *Times*, in their collective capacity have made the Government, and " left " the remaining functions to be executed within certain terri- " torial divisions called States. . . . Any individual seeking " to destroy the central Government is guilty of treason against " it, and the same thing is true of any aggregate of individuals, " even if they should constitute a majority of a State or of " several States." The *naïveté* with which these propositions are set forth, as something new to American statesmen, and the confidence with which the writer mistakes his own guesses for established facts, renders the whole argument inimitable.

So far the *Times* had pledged itself to these principles, that the South were attempting, and the North resisting, an iniquitous enterprise ; that the North were bound, not only by morality, but by considerations of expediency, to resist it ; and that under the Constitution they had the fullest legal power to resist it. It is not surprising after this that the *Times* (February 7) claims the grati- tude of the Northern States for that exhibition of English good feeling which, as it modestly anticipates, will enable them to win back the Border States, and through the Border States the South ; nor that it should (February 19) express a hope that " the force " of political cohesion will be too strong even for the ambition and

" sectional hatred of a Charleston demagogue." Mr. Lincoln or
Mr. Seward might have been satisfied with the principles of the
Times, which, indeed, though not according to knowledge, were
substantially identical with those of the Republican party. It
was rather more outspoken with regard to certain Democratic
weaknesses, although handling them with considerable tenderness,
and as to the wickedness of slavery. But for a few slips such as
that above noticed, it might have been supposed that the editor
had secured writers who had really studied the subject, and that
he was prepared to take a side founded upon some intelligible
theory. It is always, however, easy for writers of such ability as
those who form the staff of the *Times* to ape a language which
they do not really understand. Like a clever swell-mobsman in
polite society, they impose upon superficial observers ; though a
word or gesture at unguarded moments may expose the real
amount of their knowledge. During March and April, 1861,
this was illustrated by the curious perplexity induced in the *Times*
by the appearance of the tariff question. Its New York correspondent assured it that the tariff grievance was a mere blind ;
that it had been lost sight of since 1846, and was now meant as
a bid for foreign support. The *Times* hesitated. (March 5.)—Some
people, it said, thought that the slavery question was a mere
pretext. (March 8.)—However, it considered that " the North was
bringing discredit on the intrinsic merits of their cause." The
only point of similarity between this war and the war of independence was, that in both there was a dispute about customs
duties. (March 9.)—If this tariff were once out of the way, we
would soon show on which side our sympathies really are. " There
" are no disunionists," it emphatically observed, " upon this side of
" the water." (March 12.)—It roundly declares protection is "quite
as much a cause of the war as slavery:" (March 14.)—Having
heard of the compromise resolutions, it thinks that slavery is
the chief cause. Protection was mere retaliation. (March 19.)—

Slavery and tariff are on a par. (March 20.)—It inclines to the
South, because it has heard that the South are free-traders, and
intend to suppress the external slave trade. The South, however,
is reported to meditate an export duty on cotton. This " short-
sighted policy" brings the *Times* back again; and, positively
for the last time, it asserted without reservation that the North
was in the right.

Two months of complete approval of the North were thus
followed by two months of oscillation. The *Times* had "missed
stays" in going about, and was pointing in rapid succession to
any number of points of the compass. The discussion whether
slavery or tariff was the real grievance is, at best, like a discussion
whether Chichester spire fell down because the foundations were
unsound, or because a wind was blowing. The commercial
grievance was a cause, but an entirely subsidiary cause, which,
except as acting upon an incipient schism, could have produced
no effect. That the *Times* should put the slavery and the tariff
as co-ordinate causes, and that so shortly after fully stating the
case as concerns slavery, shows strikingly the shallowness of its
knowledge. Its ignorance follows not from isolated blunders,
but from a want of any theory by which the observed phenomena
may be combined into any sort of unity. It is like a rustic
looking at a volcano, and wondering whether the explosion is
caused by the fire or the smoke. The *Times* has often been compared to a weathercock, fancying that it decides the way the
wind blows. It should be added, that it is too low to feel the
more permanent currents of the atmosphere, and swings round
in obedience to every gust that eddies through Printing-house
Square.

A complete change was about to come over its spirit, and the
change nearly coincided with the fall of Fort Sumter. It distinctly
opposed the Northern claims; May 7, appeared a remarkable
article. " The North," it said, "may be justified in its denun-

" ciation of slavery, but it is not fighting for the purpose of
" driving slavery out of the land.   The South may be justified
" in protecting its independence, but that independence was not
" assailed.   Stripped of its pretexts and trappings, the war stands
" out as a mere contest for territory, or a struggle for aggrandize-
" ment.   Something may be said for either side, most for the
" North ; but nothing to justify civil war."   And, quoting the
great idol of English respectability, " Lincoln," it says, " and
" Davis have abruptly closed with an alternative at which the
" Duke of Wellington stood aghast," namely, civil war.   If an
Irish secession had broken out, and a party of Fenians seized
the forts in Cork Harbour, the Iron Duke would undoubtedly
have requested his erring brethren to part in peace.*

The change to the tone, of which the key-note was thus struck,
was the great change of the war ; and, as it was the cause of
considerable criticism, it is worth while to examine a little into
the apology put forward by the *Times* itself.

This was two-fold.   It consisted, first, of a *tu quoque.*   The
fall of Fort Sumpter startled the North out of its dream of
concession and peaceful compromise.   The *Times* had till then
been in advance even of the Northern opinion.   Its worst complaint against them had been that, owing to their democratic
institutions (January 24), they were deficient in loyalty to the
Union.   The insult to the national flag changed their spirit like
magic.   They showed an enthusiasm that amazed even their
friends.   If, to use the arguments of the *Times* itself, they had
not opposed the wicked designs of the South, if they had not
resisted the forcible subtraction of their most valuable territory,
if they had not resisted a rebellion as clearly unlawful as the
secession of Lancashire from England, the *Times* would have been

---

* The *Times* was so much pleased with this article that it reprinted many
sentences from it *verbatim* that day fortnight (May 21).   Probably it thought
that no one could remember a *Times* article for two weeks.

the first to call them poltroons and empty braggarts. As they showed unexpected spirit, the *Times* said, Pray give in at once; don't fight, whatever you do. When the Northern press complained of this sudden failure of support, the *Times* replied, You were cool when we were hot; you can't complain of us for being cool now that you are hot. You were willing (June 11) to let your erring brethren part in peace. Whilst war was preparing, you were all for conciliation. Now that your enemy has given you a slap in the face, you have actually lost your temper. It is nothing but wounded vanity (June 26). We did not cry out enough at your mighty *levée en masse;* and now you profess anger at our reasonable change. This was a calming reply.

The *Times*, however, had a much better plea, and one which it constantly put forward, in the apparent belief that it afforded a full justification. It stated (see especially October 9 and November 14) that it changed on discovering the unexpected unanimity of the South. The Border States declared for the South upon the fall of Fort Sumpter, and the *Times*, with characteristic prescience, saw that this rendered the struggle hopeless. If asserted, with every variety of vehement affirmation, that the North had no chance. I have already quoted some of these prophecies. The first, significantly enough, is on April 30. I have also given specimens from May 9, July 18, August 27, September 30, and to them I must refer. I am content to assume that the *Times* changed at the moment they saw the cause to be hopeless. It is a highly probable statement; and my only doubt of its entire accuracy arises from its positive assertion of November 26, 1860, already quoted, that the South could not hold out for sixty days. Nothing had occurred to change the military prospects, although much had occurred to change the sympathies of the *Times*. Assuming, however, for the present, that the *Times* correctly describes its reasons, I would remark that a desertion of the right side the instant you believe it to be the weaker side does not necessarily imply corrupt motives. A war which is a hopeless war is, for that reason alone, a wicked war. Advice against litigation may be perfectly judicious, although you believe that the litigant has right upon his side. But two courses remain. An honest and well-informed man who had fallen into the same blunder as the *Times* concerning Southern invincibility, would have carefully grounded his advice upon the vanity of Northern hopes. He would not have changed his opinion as to the cause or the rights of the quarrel. A weak and superficial observer, on the other hand, would be certain to make two assumptions: one, that the side which for the moment is uppermost is certain to win; the other, that the winning side is necessarily in the right. It requires deep convictions to occupy Cato's position, to hold out against the charms of the *victrix causa*. An indolent mind is glad to bring its sympathies into harmony with its expectations; it drifts imperceptibly into approbation of the conqueror's arguments as well as his strategy, and then into a belief that it always did approve of them.

Applying this test, we can speedily judge of the merits of the *Times*. And as the best gauge of its deviations from its old path, I return to the slavery question. I have shown that the *Times* started with a very fair statement as to the relations of the war to slavery. On May 23 and May 24 appeared a long article from Mr. Motley, ably reasserting the principles from which they had so strangely departed. The *Times* would have none of it. It had said (March 28) that the only "point of contact" between this war and the war of independence was, that there were customs duties in both. Now it asserted, May 23, that the spirit of George III. had entered into the Northern people; and May 24, it repeated, in opposition to Mr. Motley, that the precedent of George III. was applicable. "The North," it said, "seems to have a good cause, but it is surprisingly like the cause of England." It had gone further in an article by which Mr. Motley's letter was probably provoked. The war, it had said (May 11), was not one about slavery, but merely " to keep slavery as one of the social " elements of the Union. . . It was a war to keep Southern " debtors and their property from getting beyond the grasp " of Northern merchants." This ingenious theory completely turned the tables, and, as I shall show, was a favourite opinion of the *Times*. Presently, however, the *Times* made another change. Mrs. Beecher Stowe had made an appeal to the anti-slavery sentiment of the English people.

She said, very truly, that it was "an anti-slavery war, not in " form but in fact ;" that "national existence and not emancipa-" tion was the announced battle-cry; but national existence was " in this case felt to imply the extinction of slavery." (These words, though expressing a sentiment now commonplace, illustrate the great difficulty of the American Government. To obtain foreign sympathy, they must have proclaimed a crusade against slavery; but, for the all-important purpose of securing unity at home, it was necessary to make love of the Union the watch-word, as, indeed, it was the efficient motive.) The *Times* (September 9) quotes these remarks in Mrs. Stowe's own words, because it would " scruple to attribute to her views so little worthy of the authoress of *Uncle Tom's Cabin.*" Mrs. Stowe, as it condescends to inform her, "has mistaken an electioneering cry for the war-note of a crusade." And with a ludicrous pomposity it lays down its own opinion. It was not " an accident," it admits, that the fracture took place at the point of juncture between slave and free States, though, if we define an accident to be an event whose cause is undiscoverable, it is hard to say what else it could be. The *Times*, however, continues :—
" That this was not the true object of the movement on either " side, admits of every proof short of demonstration ; that the " slavery question has since been lost sight of in the *mêlée* of civil " war admits of actual demonstration." Ten days before this was

written (August 31) Fremont's proclamation freeing the slaves of disloyal owners had already been issued; and by all who had eyes to see (including Mr. Russell, the *Times'* special correspondent) was felt to be the first step towards an inevitable conflict.   Upon hearing of this proclamation the *Times* sapiently remarked (September 30), as if it was a novel, but not improbable, theory, that some people considered abolition to be at the bottom of the whole business.   Without committing itself to this or the opposite opinion, it added that it was highly probable that abolition would be adopted as a war measure—not a very rash prediction, after abolition had actually commenced in Missouri, but a singular comment on its " demonstration " three weeks before that slavery had been already lost sight of.

The fullest confession of faith that I can find is contained in a review (January 14, 1862) of Mr. Spence's work—a book remarkable for its power of varnishing over the ordinary Southern arguments with a thin coating of sham philosophy. The *Times* adopted his conclusions, and spoke (April 26, 1862) afterwards of Mr. Spence's "admirable work" as clearing up the subject.   The *Times*, following Mr. Spence, complacently attributes the war to the demoralization of the Northern people.   That that demoralization, if it were proved to exist, should be ever spoken of by Englishmen, except in a tone of regret and humiliation, I consider to be a disgrace to the speaker. If millions of English-speaking people, brought up in the enjoyment of our laws, literature, and religion, are, indeed, corrupt to the core, we should repent in sackcloth and ashes.   The *Times*, however, talks the usual talk about democracy, reckons up the burning of slaves, Lynch law, bullying in Congress, and other direct products of the slave power, as part of the Northern iniquities, and finally reduces the causes of the war to three heads.   The first is the change in the political balance due to emigration; the second, an "original antipathy" aggravated by

Abolitionists; the third, the protective policy of the North. To repeat what I have already said, none of these causes can even be fully stated except as corollaries to the slavery question. Emigrants are naturally attracted by free labour; protective tariffs injured East Tennessee or Illinois as much as Eastern Virginia or South Carolina, but they only alienated the slave States. As for the " original antipathy," the statement about Abolitionists is sufficient to prove that it means an antipathy between free men and slaveholders. The *Times,* however, argues that slavery is of no importance. " The reader will observe the " clear distinction between slavery itself and the agitation " for its abolition "—two things which I should have thought it impossible to confound. The *Times,* however, means in a blundering way to point out what it afterwards states as follows : " As a cause of secession, slavery is subordinate. . . . It " may be the reel on which the evil has been wound; but it is " not the material of which the coil is made ; it is a delusion, if " not a fraud, to represent it otherwise." I don't quite understand the metaphor, but its general purport is plain enough.

The *Times* had thus asserted within a year that slavery was the cause of the war; that slavery was one cause and protection another; that slavery was the cause and protection a pretext; that slavery had little to do with the war and protection much; that it could be "all but demonstrated " that slavery had nothing to do with it at first, and "quite demonstrated" that slavery had since passed out of sight; that "some people thought" that abolition was at the bottom of the whole business, and that it would very probably be the result ; and that slavery was the "reel on which " the coil was wound," though " not the material of which the coil " was made." In other words, the *Times* knew nothing about it. I shall show directly that its opinions as to the effect of the war upon slavery were equally oscillating.

V.—The " Times " on the True Cause of the War.

I must at first, however, remark upon the attempts which the *Times* made to account for the war, leaving slavery out of the question.   After such dogged determination to prove that the magazine did not blow up on account of the powder, it was bound to invent some other cause.   For the *Times* always affects the philosophical.   Preserving its equilibrium by a series of oscillations, it never falls into the fanaticism of either extreme. It eschewed the violent abuse of the Tory organs—except when abuse was really required—as religiously as it eschewed abolitionist declamations.   " *Surtout point de zèle* " was its motto, or, in other words, " no political principles at any price."   Hence, the *Times* had to discover some working explanation of the war not involving slavery.   It could not adopt the servant-maid's excuse that the vase " came broken," and the " three causes " enumerated by Mr. Spence were, of course, too absurd to be ever seriously mentioned again.

In the first place the *Times* said, as a philosopher is bound to say, that the separation was owing to far deeper causes than slavery.   After pooh-poohing those shallow observers who could believe that a war between slaveholders and non-slaveholders might be in some way connected with slavery, it said boldly —(May 30, 1861)—" the inhabitants of the North and those of the South are two distinct peoples " of the same stock, as much opposed " as the Austrians to the Italians, or the Muscovites to the Poles."   To test such assertions they should be inverted : it would be a singular remark that the Germans differed from the Italians as much as the people of East from those of Middle Tennessee.   (Sept. 19, 1861.)—It proceeded to moralize upon this. The tendency in Europe is, it appears, rather " for large States to split asunder than for small ones to be consolidated," as may be seen in France and Italy.   The cause of this tendency is that

" nationality " is the great modern feeling. North and South have separated, because North and South have as little in common as Magyar and German. The logic of this is equal to the accuracy of its facts. If nationality is the ruling principle, North and South should keep together. The *Times* can only say roundly that they differ as much as Magyar and German. It never condescends to specify the differences which separate races identical in blood, language, religion, laws, and a few other characteristics, and for many years bound together in the same political and social organizations. A year later—(Jan. 23, 1863)—the *Times* repeats its statement that slavery is only part of the difference, but, as before, it declines to state the other part. Some better explanation was required.

One might have supposed that the *Times* would have set the war down to that universal cause of all modern political events —democracy. People are apt to fancy that the mere mention of democracy gives them claims to be De Tocquevilles. The *Times* felt the temptation ; but there were two objections to its yielding to it : first, democracy would not account for the precise line taken by the split, and was so far an irrelevant cause logically ; secondly, the *Times* is a Liberal paper. Accordingly, it adopted its usual plan of both asserting and denying democracy to be the cause. People are apt to declare themselves to be miserable sinners, and to deny that they have broken any one of the Ten Commandments in particular. By an inverse method, the *Times* denies in general terms that democracy was the cause of the war. In detail it constantly lays the blame upon the crimes generally associated with democracy.

" We," says the *Times* of April 28, 1862, " were never amongst " those who exulted over the alleged breakdown of democratic insti- " tutions ; we saw from the first that it was not so much democracy " as the principle of Federalism, under very peculiar conditions, " that was on its trial." It had asserted more distinctly still

(September 25, 1861), that it agreed with its correspondent, that the war was not traceable to democracy, and that it has not been forced by the mob upon the educated classes.

A fortnight before (September 12, 1861), in an argument which ingeniously combined various classes of blunders, it remarks :— " We say nothing of the sacrifice of free institutions, &c. &c., " and certainly nothing of gentlemen being ridden out of town " on a rail. King Mob, where he is supreme, will naturally " require the same agent as any single tyrant." However, the *Times* hopes that the war will soon stop, because the mob in New York and elsewhere are already feeling the pressure of hunger.

May 24, 1861.—It had kindly remarked, that though the Southern statesmen could not be justified by any rule of law in breaking up the Union, law has not been the rule commonly prevailing in America, but "almost unrestrictedly the rule of self-will." In flat contradiction to the assertion of September 25, just quoted, it had said on August 14, 1861, " The war is the " result of mob passions, and the real act of men who have " comparatively little interest in the maintenance of union, order, " national credit, or property itself."

The two lines are ingeniously combined in one article by artifice of which the *Times* is specially fond.

" Far be it from us," it says (October 18, 1861), "to dogma- " tize about democracy, or to attribute the civil war to " republican institutions. The secession of the South is certainly " not a necessary result of any form of government. Yet " it is not too much to say that the form which democracy " has taken for the last thirty years, or since the Presidency " of Jackson, was likely to lead to such a result." In other words, we won't distinctly say it, but we will hint it. It is common for Protestant advocates to disclaim any wish to impute deliberate lying to Roman Catholics; but, they insinuate, if Roman Catholics did wish for an excuse, they might know where to find it.

It appears, I think, pretty plainly that the *Times* was in the position described by Mr. Tennyson, " sitting apart, holding no form of creed, but contemplating all," and, indeed, trying on each in turn. It did not really think that democracy was the cause of the war, but it could not help saying stinging things about democrats ; it could not doubt that slavery had really something to do with it, but it tried by every means to evade the inevitable conclusion. Slavery was an awkward topic, and it went so far as it dared, which sometimes was very far indeed, in denying it to be involved in the quarrel.

VI.—THE " TIMES " ON THE SLAVERY QUESTION.

I will now trace shortly the treatment applied by the *Times* to the successive phases of the slavery question. It will appear, I think, that it did not escape the nemesis common to all apologists for slavery. The Southern Confederacy fell because, in the words of its Vice-President, it was grounded upon the cornerstone of slavery. Their advocates have confuted themselves over and over again by the strange contortions of argument forced upon them by the necessity of concealing this part of their client's case. They were constantly impaled upon the horn of a dilemma ; they were bound to maintain either that slavery was a good thing, and that the South were fighting for it; or that slavery was a bad thing, and the Southern cause had nothing to do with it. The first assertion shocked the consciences of Englishmen, and the second their common-sense. As the war proceeded, each proposition became more untenable. By degrees, the change of opinion, which had been predicted by all impartial observers, developed itself. The temporizing and half-hearted dropped out, and the lead gradually fell into the hands of the extreme of each party. The *Times*, indeed, admitted, as I have remarked, that abolition might be adopted as a war measure; and, after the event, it observed upon the transference of power to the most thorough-going partisans as a process naturally to be expected. But, as a rule, the *Times* showed its perception by asserting that the reverse of this process was taking place.

Thus (Dec. 14, 1861), it observes, in answer to Mr. Sumner, that the commercial classes in America depend upon slavery for cotton, sugar, and tobacco, and are, therefore, interested in maintaining it. Any opposition to slavery would divide the North into two parts—a good specimen of the method of reasoning from *à priori* considerations.

July 28, 1862.—It observes that, "So soon as it becomes " evident that the South cannot be retained as a slave-owning " portion of the Union, New York must naturally be against any " further prosecution of the war—as also will be Massachusetts " and Pennsylvania. . . . If Pennsylvania cannot sell her " manufactures to the South, and New York cannot be the " banker and broker of the planters" (which would, it supposes, follow from abolition), " their interest in the Union is gone. " This accounts for the decay of the Union feeling in the Atlantic " cities." And it frequently propounded a theory stated as follows (Feb. 16, 1863). One consequence of the emancipation policy is becoming evident. " The war, instead of crushing down " the revolt of the South, has produced a movement for secession " within what remained of the Union. Political opinion in the " North-Western States is ripening to revolt."

I may therefore assume it to be the settled conviction of the *Times* (that is, an opinion which it does not flatly contradict oftener than three or four times), that emancipation policy, instead of being that to which the North would inevitably become reconciled, was likely to be the source of further schisms. But the *Times* was not contented with proving that the policy of emancipation was disintegrating the remnant of the Union; it insisted upon also proving at intervals that it was a perfectly nugatory pretext, and in process of abandonment by its authors. It was, doubtless, so anxious to get this awkward topic well buried, that it almost believed in the fulfilment of its wishes. Thus (September 9, 1861), it asserted, as I have remarked, that it would be proved to demonstration that slavery had gone out of sight.

April 3, 1863.—"Wholesale emancipation has ceased to rally the Republicans themselves." In place of it, a more genuine sentiment is appealed to ; "a demand for the Union at any price, " whatever the effect on slavery. It is thus that we interpret the " spread of Union Leagues. Abolition is to be excluded from their " platform, because it has been tried as a political engine and " found wanting." "The proclamation will be virtually repu- " diated just as it has begun to bear its fatal fruits."

Nov. 14, 1863.—"The tenor of Lincoln's proclamation has " been well understood by the coloured people. There is no " disposition to desert the cause of the whites, and, furthermore, " the idea of conquering the South by means of negro troops has " been utterly abandoned."

Sept. 19, 1864.—It assures us, in an article to which I shall refer presently, 'that slavery is "no longer a point at issue, and will not be interfered with, after peace is restored."

The *Times* being thus eager to prove that emancipation was a policy which could not unite the North, and which was always being abandoned, though it persisted in always returning to life, it is curious to ask what it supposed to be the probable effect of the war upon slavery. I will quote a few passages to prove how plainly it had realized the bearings of this complicated question :—

May 9, 1862.—"The Union is impossible except upon the " basis of slavery ; division is incompatible with the permanent " existence of slavery."

Or, as it still more emphatically asserted—

October 7, 1862.—"We are in Europe thoroughly convinced
" that the death of slavery must follow as necessarily upon the
" success of the Confederates in this war as the dispersion of
" darkness upon the rising sun."

March 26, 1863.—Appeared an elaborate article, in which it is
proved that, if the war fails, the South will become a great slave
empire. "No doubt it would carry the institution of slavery into
" all its new territory, whether conquered or annexed, whether on
" the mainland or on the isles of the sea."

To explain this startling contradiction in terms of all that it
had been hitherto saying, I must remark that the success of the
South about this time had emboldened the *Times* to plant itself
upon the more dangerous horn of the dilemma I have mentioned,
and to declare that the South was fighting for slavery and that
slavery was a good thing. "The race," it said, "vegetates
" in Africa, it rises to something better in the Southern
" States of America, it languishes in the Northern States, it has
" died out in this country." Though it may not be well off any-
where, it is at its best in the South.

Dec. 18, 1863.—It is remarked that "if the Southern resistance
is finally subdued, the institution will probably cease to exist."

Let me sum up these opinions. The *Times* "demonstrated,"
in September 1861, in a passage already quoted, that slavery had
gone out of sight already, and was in no way affected by the
war. In the first two passages quoted above it asserts that
slavery will be destroyed if the North fail, and preserved if they
succeed. In the last two it asserts that slavery will be preserved
if the North fails and destroyed if they succeed. One other
variation of opinion is possible, namely—that slavery will perish
in any case. This view was elaborately maintained in an article
of March 24, 1864. "It is very remarkable," it naively observes,
" that the most conspicuous result of the American war is the
" gradual elevation of the black race in social and political

" position. As happens in all political revolutions, the most
" thoroughgoing party has proved the most enduring, and that
" party is the Abolitionist." If the restoration of the Union is
hopeless, the destruction of slavery is not so. " It was pointed
" out, indeed, at a very early period of the war, that slavery
" could hardly escape from the double danger by which it was
" threatened. If the North were victorious they could do what
" they chose." ˙ (This, as it carefully explained, April 26, 1862,
must be either the extirpation or expulsion of the blacks.)
" If the South, they would be surrounded by free soil " (but, as
shown, March 26, 1863, a slave power including " the Isles of
the Sea "); and it proceeds to argue that the South will, by arming
the slaves, obtain a numerical majority for the first time in the
war. Perhaps the most direct contradiction to this article is the
one of April 26, 1862, just quoted, where it is explained that the
best chance for the negro is for the South to succeed, in which
case the negroes will remain slaves as before. The same land
will not hold the emancipated black and the slaveholding white.
" The blacks must be re-enslaved, must be exterminated, or must
" be re-expelled." Should the North conquer, the question will
be between the last two alternatives.

VII.—The " Times " on Emancipation Measures.

I will conclude the subject of slavery by showing the nature of
the criticism applied by the *Times* to the most prominent of the
successive measures which marked the gradual adoption of an
anti-slavery policy. Although the accumulated effect of those
measures was too conspicuous to be evaded, it was just possible
to misrepresent each taken separately. As we shall presently see
that, according to the *Times*, the greatest military successes of the
North were obtained by an unbroken series of defeats, it will appear
that the old stronghold of slavery was stormed in a series of
assaults, each of which was a dishonest feint or a step backwards.

In the beginning of 1862, Mr. Lincoln brought forward a plan for assisting any State to emancipate its slaves. He proposed that Congress should help in compensating the owners. If, he said, "the border States accepted this plan, slavery would be doomed, and the cause of the war removed."

The *Times* argued (March 24, 1862) that the plan was absurd. Slavery, it said, was still kept up in the district of Columbia, Maryland, Tennessee, Virginia, Kentucky, and Missouri. (I have not been fortunate enough to find any recognition in the *Times* of the subsequent abolition of slavery in four of the five States named.) Hence, by some process of logic which is far beyond me, it inferred that "Mr. Lincoln has begun to entertain the idea "so firmly entertained by every European politician that the only "possible solution of the struggle is entire separation between "North and South." I cannot, I say, follow the argument, but I am not surprised that the *Times* pronounces the scheme to be totally unintelligible.

It soon became evident that the scheme was not to be carried out. The *Times* then said (August 8, 1862) that Mr. Lincoln had wished to convert the border States into free-soil States, "well knowing and indeed avowing that the result of such a "revolution would be their final detachment from the side of the "South. The proposal itself was discreetly framed; . . . "by such a decision the border States would have committed "themselves to the principle of abolition, and have broken with "slavery and the South once for all."

The *Times* characteristically shrank from admitting to itself the obvious nature of the proposal until the discovery that it was not to be practically tested.

In October, 1862, Mr. Lincoln announced that he should issue his emancipation proclamation in the beginning of 1863. He recommended at the same time to Congress a scheme for the compensation of loyal owners. As this great measure was

perhaps the most important step, and the crowning glory of
Mr. Lincoln's life, I will venture to recall to notice one or two
obvious facts which the *Times* systematically disregarded. The
Northern generals had in the first instance so scrupulously
abstained from interference with slavery, that they even restored
slaves to rebel owners. General Butler hit upon the happy legal
discovery that these slaves were " contraband of war ; " whence
arose the slang term of " contrabands " as applied to negroes.
Now President Lincoln's proclamation was an extensive application of General Butler's argument. Its constitutionality may be
disputed, but its justification was based simply upon the right of
a commander-in-chief to appropriate the property of belligerents
opposed to him. The very arguments, therefore, by which it was
justified proved it to be inapplicable to the loyal States. Mr.
Lincoln had no shadow of legal claim to emancipate their slaves
any more than to seize their cattle, and he never in any instance
put forward such a claim. As, at the same time, the emancipation
of slaves in the planting States rendered slavery in the border
States insecure, some measure for securing compensation to loyal
owners, or to those who might submit before the proclamation came
into action, was a natural complement to the proclamation. As a
military measure, the proclamation struck at the weakest point of
the enemy. The policy which it officially sanctioned was, in
fact, forced upon the North by the logic of events. Wherever
the Northern armies went, they freed the slaves at the cannon's
mouth, and the proclamation confirmed and accepted the result.
It acted like an acid, softening the hard shell of Southern society,
enabling the bayonet to penetrate. Southern society was, for the
time, disorganized, to be reconstituted on a different basis. In
the fact of that reconstitution lay the moral justification of the
Northern enterprise, for it permitted the hope that the success
won by arms might be consolidated by removing the very cause
of irritation. The Northern armies administered a medicine

potent enough, not merely to remove the symptoms, but to renew
the constitution of the patient.   But did not the proclamation
incite to a servile war?   In one sense it did, and in that sense
a servile war is the holiest of all wars.   If a man may not fight to
raise himself from the level of a beast of burden to that of a man,
it is hard to say for what cause he may fight.   How is a man
ever to be justified for shooting his fellow-men, if he may not
shoot them when they have prevented him from marrying, from
being educated, from receiving the wages of labour, and from all
the rights of property?   But, it is said, a servile war often leads
to frightful atrocities.   The brutified man takes the vengeance of
a brute upon those who have degraded him.   Massacres and
outrages will follow the rebound from a fearful wrong ;   and holy
as the cause may be, it may be accompanied by horrors so great
as to quench our sympathy and to make us think the liberty of a
race too dearly bought by such sufferings of one generation.

   If, then, the war can be so organized as to be freed from these
stains, if slaves fighting for freedom commit no more outrages
than men fighting for commerce or for a diplomatic point of
honour, they have the most imperative of all claims upon our
sympathy.   Before we refuse it, we should be certain that the
horrors incidentally resulting will more than outweigh the blessings.
But it is an admirable topic for thoughtless abuse to charge upon
the abettors of a servile war all the atrocities that we instinctively
associate with the name.   It is easy to slur over the fact that
such atrocities have not, in fact, occurred, and were not invited or
provoked.   Now, the warfare sanctioned by the proclamation
was, I may unhesitatingly say, obnoxious to no such objections.
Even their enemies have not attributed any special brutalities to
the negro troops.   They were less inclined to breaches of discipline than their white comrades.   Nor, again, was the proclamation at any time intended to provoke a servile warfare of the
atrocious kind ; for the policy adopted simultaneously was, not to

endeavour to raise the blacks in distant plantations, but to form brigades, of fugitive slaves on territory belonging to the Union. Neither was there any probability that the proclamation would unintentionally lead to sporadic insurrections in the South. For, besides that the proclamation could scarcely reach the remote plantations, it would be manifestly far more natural for a discontented negro to run off to a place where he could obtain arms and be effectually drilled, than to rise "promiscuously" in the midst of a population armed to the teeth. The proclamation tended to discourage such risings by promising a safe asylum for fugitives. The evident purpose of the proclamation, confirmed by all we know of the circumstances under which it was issued, of its plain meaning, and of the means by which it was carried out, was simply to give a legal sanction to a policy enforced by military, moral, and political considerations. Experience has confirmed this view, and it is, even at the present moment, the charter under which the negroes of the Southern States claim a right to freedom.

I will quote a few passages to show how the *Times* treated the measure to which, more than any other, is owing the most remarkable social revolution of our time.

Oct. 7, 1862.—Lincoln has declared that after January 1, 1863, "neither he nor his army will do anything to suppress *any* " efforts which the negroes of the Southern States may make for " the recovery of their freedom. This means, of course, that " Mr. Lincoln will, on the 1st of January next, do his best to " excite a servile war in the States which he cannot occupy with " his armies. . . . He will seek out the places which are left " but slightly guarded, and where the women and children have " been trusted to the fidelity of coloured domestics. He will " appeal to the black blood of the African. He will whisper of " the pleasures of slaughter, and the gratification of yet fiercer " instincts, and when blood begins to flow and shrieks come " piercing through the darkness, Mr. Lincoln will wait till the

" rising flames tell that all is consummated, and then he will rub
" his hands and think that revenge is sweet." . . . " The
" South will answer with a hiss of scorn." New York
and Pennsylvania will become disloyal if slavery goes. " If
" Lincoln wants such a conquest as this, the North is perhaps
" yet strong enough to conquer Hayti." It is a mere proof of
" impotent malignity," although there may be some " partial
" risings; for if any power publish an exhortation to the labouring
" classes of a community to plunder and murder, it will meet
" with some response."

Oct. 14.—The proclamation is an incitement to assassination.
" In truth, it is nothing else, and can mean nothing else."

Oct. 21.—After some facetiousness about " Lincoln the Last,"
after pointing out that though " Honest Abe " had been honest
to his party, he had been dishonest to his country, and
how honesty in this sense (perhaps in some others) was an intolerable evil and a sufficient provocation to secession, and inferring
" how insupportable must be despotism of which a man of this calibre
" is despot," it inquires, " Is Lincoln yet a name not known to us
" as it will be known to posterity? Is it ultimately to be classed
" among the catalogue of monsters, wholesale assassins, and
" butchers of their kind?" The *Times* thus charged Mr. Lincoln,
in bombast worthy of the *Family Herald*, with all sorts of
atrocities. There was, however, a fear that some weak haters of
slavery on this side of the Atlantic might be attracted by the
name of emancipation, and, indeed, a crowded meeting was held
in Exeter Hall, and the sympathies of the English anti-slavery
party were manifestly afflicted.

The Northern cause was so distinctly identifying itself with
the profession of anti-slavery opinions that the *Times* could only
take one of two courses. Either it might deny that slavery was
an evil, or it might assert that the North was merely hypocritical
in its assault. As usual, it did both. The first course required

some courage. It made a bold stroke on January 6, 1863, in answer to some of the American Abolitionists. "They preach," says the *Times*, "with the Bible in their hands. In that book " there is not one single text that can be perverted to prove " that slavery is unlawful, though there is much which naturally " tends to its mitigation, its elevation, and its final extinction." It then repeats the common special pleading as to St. Paul's Epistle to Philemon. " The only possible doubt about the exact " meaning of his advice is whether slaves are to refuse their " liberty even if it be offered, or whether they are merely to " remain true to their masters even if chance presents oppor- " tunity of escape. . . . If it be said that slavery is at " variance with the spirit of the Gospel, so are a good many " things which are not yet laid under a ban of abolition or " threatened with the war-power," *e.g.* purple and fine linen and good clerical incomes.

This article marks, I believe, the point at which the *Times* culminated. The amount of its anti-slavery sentiments at a given time is determined by the variations in the Northern tide of success. This was just after the battle of Fredericksburg. This defence of slavery—or attack upon biblical morality—was, however, a little too much for the British public, and the *Times* retired towards its former position, that slavery was "in truth a hateful and horrible thing," though it still vigorously denounced emancipation. The palpable failure of this policy—for the article produced a general cry of disgust—led it to take the safer line of declaring that the North was not in earnest.

The *Times* therefore asserted (January 19, 1863) that the whole affair was a piece of hypocrisy intended for foreign consumption. " All the actors," it said, "are anxious to tell each other that this " proclamation is Buncombe," specially Lincoln, but " no one in " England imagines that the President . . . . desires emanci-

" pation for itself." (No human being would now dare to doubt it.) The *Times* speaks of itself as hating slavery, but being " unmoved by all the stage-tricks of Mr. Lincoln and his friends." " Mr. Bright is not such a simpleton as to believe in the " benevolent intentions of Mr. Lincoln. Mr. Adams must have " laughed heartily with himself at the few woodcocks who have " been caught in his springes." This last polished sarcasm refers to an address from the Anti-Slavery Society, congratulating Mr. Adams on the proclamation.

Feb. 6, 1863.—"Of all the hypocrisies," it says, "which have " scandalized the world within our memory, the pretext that this " war is being carried on for the benefit of the negro" (no one asserted that it was carried on primarily for his benefit) "is the " greatest. It is a gross palpable imposture." An army of 150,000 negroes having been mentioned : " We all know what " that means ; it means 10,000 domestic tragedies, and a political " sham which seeks to perpetrate a hideous crime."

Feb. 19.—The Anti-Slavery Society is compared to a society for the abolition of captivity in the Zoological Gardens ; and, continuing in this vein of metaphor, their leaders are said to be small dogs barking in the dens of the old lions Wilberforce and Clarkson. This will probably be a sufficient specimen of the *Times'* abuse. I will notice one or two palpable misrepresentations of a similar class.

Oct 7, 1862.—"Where he has no power," says the *Times*, " Mr. Lincoln will set the negroes free ; where he retains power, " he will consider them to be slaves."

I need not enlarge upon the absurdity of this constantly repeated statement. It depends upon a blundering notion that Mr. Lincoln had claimed power to abolish slavery or to free slaves on other than military grounds. In direct contradiction to the *Times*, it may be said that Mr. Lincoln freed the slaves where he had the legal power, and, of course, did not free them where he had not. But the *Times* systematically refused to see this.

Dec. 17.—It is amazed at a man, as autocratic as " the Czar," talking about Constitutional amendments. " The scheme," it says, " is very unlike the proclamation of three months since. It is a laboured substitute for the edict of September last." The fact is that it was a natural corollary, as I have shown.

Dec. 29, 1862.—It asserts that the Northern Government is inconsistent, because, while seeking to identify the North in the eyes of foreign Powers with the cause of emancipation, it offered " the retention of their slaves as a premium to loyal slave- " holders." That is, it did not attempt forcibly, and in defiance of all law and policy, to deprive them of their slaves, without offering compensation. To twist the non-infliction of a severe penalty into the offer of a " premium " is an ingenious logical feat. But the *Times* capped even this blunder.

It had been reported that Southern troops had shot certain negroes taken in arms. The *Times* (January 21, 1863) ingeniously remarked that Mr. Lincoln's abolition decree was fortunately illogical enough to give the negro security. " Under " the Federal flag he is a slave with all the immunities of the " servile condition." " If he can be held as a slave by one side, " and shot as a free man by the other, his position is miserable " indeed." There is something so muddleheaded about this, that I rather fear to put any interpretation upon it. It appears, however, to be the impression of the writer that any slave freed by Mr. Lincoln's proclamation immediately became a slave again on entering the Union lines, and was probably tossed up for by the first white regiment he met. If the *Times* did not mean this, its remarks are sheer nonsense. If it did, they are not materially better.

To conclude the subject of the proclamation, I will quote one or two further passages on its effect. I have already quoted a remarkable one of March 24, 1864, on the " gradual elevation of the black race," which, however, the *Times* appears to think a mere accident.

June 18, 1863.—It says, " We shall be surprised if the presence " of black regiments be not found a heavy loss to the present " army, and a grievous loss to the enlistment of a new one." Within a week (June 23, 1863), it admits that the consequences of the emancipation measure are becoming "important enough," the enlistment of negroes being in progress in Louisiana. This admission seems to be made to prove that horrible atrocities will result.

Certain atrocities were soon reported, but practised not by, but on, negro troops. Mr. Lincoln answered by a declaration that if the Confederates massacred black prisoners he must retaliate. The *Times* admits (August 17, 1863) that he could not do otherwise, but lectures him on the wickedness of the proclamation which made such measures necessary. Don't call in a policeman, or you may make the mob angry.

It declared (I have already quoted some passages) that the policy was a failure, and speedily to be abandoned. (December 31, 1863.)—It asserts that "Mr. Lincoln's proclamation has not " fulfilled the hopes of its authors, because it has not caused the " servile insurrection which was justly deprecated by its opponents' " policy." It admits that large numbers of slaves have been liberated, though, by the army, and not by the proclamation, and adds, " if the Southern resistance is finally subdued, the institution will probably cease to exist." In other words, it admits that all its own predictions as to the probable effect of the proclamation have been falsified—that no atrocities have resulted, and that slavery is being extinguished. As for the quibble about the " army," the very purpose of the proclamation was to legalize the action of the army. But, whilst admitting that Mr. Lincoln's avowed expectations have come true, and its own been falsified, it persists in attributing to him other intentions of secret malignity which have been disappointed.

The candour of this article, which is one of the annual sum
maries of the *Times*, corresponds to a certain superiority in its tone.
It soon relapsed. (January 5, 1864.)—Mr. Lincoln having stated
that 100,000 negroes were already in the military service, the *Times*
coolly assumed that not more than 100,000 had been liberated in all.
The falsehood of this may be guessed from the fact that their
own correspondent (January 29) tried to prove that not more
than half a million negroes had been freed. I am not aware
that the *Times* ever retracted its error, but it found a more
convenient line of argument by asserting, not that the North had
no negro troops, but (February 17) that their armies were entirely
composed of negroes and foreigners.

I will give two further illustrations of the candour of the *Times*
in this matter of slavery. Society being thoroughly disorganized
in Louisiana, General Banks put out a scheme for establishing
temporary relations between freedmen and their former masters.
I need not argue as to whether the scheme was carried out in good
faith, nor whether it was to be considered as a step backwards
towards slavery or forwards towards freedom. I will only remark
that it clearly defined an intermediate state of things. The chief
points in which Banks's regulations made the freedman differ
from the slave were these : the freedmen were to have a right to
schools, to a piece of ground for themselves, to wages at a fixed
rate, to choose their own masters, to receive support from
Government if incapable. They were not to be flogged, and
could not be sold or separated from their families. No one
regulation can be mentioned which placed them at a disadvantage
as compared with slaves.

The *Times* quietly asserts (March 3, 1864), that this scheme is
in substance identical with slavery, and by May 17 maintains that
it has restored slavery in an aggravated form. Between these two
days (March 24) occurs its proof that the most conspicuous result
of the war is the elevation of the black race.

By the end of 1864 it was abundantly evident that the war was crushing out slavery. Mr. Seward took advantage of this to say that slavery was no longer in question. Both Republicans and Democrats might, as he said, look upon abolition as an accomplished fact.

The *Times* hereupon said (September 19, 1864), after quoting his assertion that slavery was no longer at issue : " The Republicans " have played with slavery, as they have played with other " questions." Lincoln thought the Abolitionists might be useful, and went so far as to make abolition (in his message to the delegates in Canada) a condition for the readmission of the South. (I need hardly add that he never swerved from this.) The *Times* proceeds to say that Seymour denounced him, and Seward has followed suit ; it denies that slavery was any longer the point at issue, and says that it would not be interfered with after peace was restored. It quotes Mr. Seward's speech in the same sense —(November 26).

That is, Mr. Seward said that a stipulation for killing slavery was useless, because slavery, if not dead, was mortally wounded. The *Times* made him say that a stipulation was not required, because he did not care whether it lived or died.

I have done with the mass of contradicting utterances concerning slavery. Let me draw one or two conclusions. I do not set this down to malice, for malice would be more consistent. The *Times* vacillates too much to obey the great commandment : " Tell a lie and stick to it." It rather proves, what no one doubts to be the case, that the *Times* takes in its politics as improvident people take in their coals, by the day, and has little thought either for the morrow or for the day before. Its only consistent effort was to avoid the unpleasant necessity of allowing that slavery was concerned. As it had drifted, from various causes, into a general attitude of hostility to the American people, it would not make the most obvious admissions of a Northern tendency. Yet if the *Times* had given the devil his due, it might have attacked him with more force. Its line of argument would have been more consistent and had more appearance of candour. It might have made a tolerable case out of the States' Rights argument, had it not been obliged always to exhibit itself in the attitude of one wriggling out of an awkward dilemma. A little honesty would have paid in the long run. The British public were quite prepared to hear the truth about slavery, and the *Times* would have gained in reputation from the unwonted credit of sticking to the truth when the truth was under a cloud. It ought to be honest even with a view to its reputation; to quote its own courteous language, would it not be well for it to think sometimes what "ought" means?

VIII.—THE "TIMES" CORRESPONDENCE.

I have shown into what perplexity the *Times* was thrown by its constant misconception of the relations of slavery to the origin of the war. It would not admit that slavery was in any sense the cause of the war, or, I should rather say that, after its conversion in 1861, it would only make that admission in one of its occasional paroxysms of self-contradiction—and, at the same time, it could allege no other cause. I shall now endeavour to point out how much the same error distorted its view of all subsequent facts.

The *Times* was, I believe, more honest than most persons suppose, because it was more ignorant than common readers can easily be persuaded to believe. It is, therefore, necessary to explain, before proceeding further, the process by which its judgment on American affairs was apparently formed, as I cannot otherwise do justice to either its ignorance or its honesty. The *Times* began by sending out to America a gentleman for whose impartiality and powers of description every one must feel a high respect. During 1861, his letters, although in my opinion frequently expressing erroneous judgments, were highly graphic, interesting, and invariably gentlemanlike. Mr. Russell, however, left America in the spring of 1862, on not being permitted to accompany M'Clellan's peninsular expedition. Occasional letters were afterwards published from a Southern correspondent, of whom I shall only say that a little more information, with a few less sentimentalities about Lee and Jackson, would have improved the substance of his writing, thought they might have made his presence less acceptable to the Southern authorities. From the moment at which he commenced his letters, he became (if he had not previously been) a thorough partizan of the Southern cause. The *Times* also employed a special correspondent during part of 1863 and 1864. His letters were unfavourable to the North, but evidently candid, and, therefore, such as no Northern sympathiser should condemn. From the beginning of 1862 until the present year, the *Times* has maintained at New York another correspondent. It had been originally my intention to treat this gentleman's letters at some length. I do not, however, think them worth the labour, because they are in themselves feeble, and because the degree to which the *Times* is responsible for them may be doubted. I will in a few words give my impression of them, because, as will presently appear, they had considerable influence upon the *Times'* official articles.

I read (November 12, 1863) a letter from New York in which the word " heroism " caught my eye, as applied to the North. On looking more closely, I saw that in the same sentence the North was called " stiffnecked " and " stubborn," and that, after all, it only possessed an amount of consistency and unity " which really resembled heroism." Still I thought it scarcely possible that the New York correspondent should have permitted himself such a slip, and on looking more closely, I found that the letter came from the " special correspondent " above mentioned. This anecdote will illustrate the general tendency of these remarkable letters. They are one long effort, lasting for three years, to shut his own eyes and the eyes of his countrymen to the existence of any heroic qualities in the people amongst whom he lived. It must have been an irksome task for a generous mind, and it is nothing short of sickening for any man of common feeling to read as a collected whole. We might take it as an agreeable bitter at intervals, but any one who follows my example in plodding through column after column of ceaseless abuse of a great nation will rise with a sense of weariness and disgust. Every patriotic action is explained to have really originated in corruption or selfishness. Scandal after scandal is raked together, and carefully exhibited as an average specimen of American affairs. If you put any faith in the writer, the whole political and social machinery is rotten at the core and is worked by the most degraded motives; America is peopled by an unprincipled mob, sprinkled with charlatans and hypocrites, and governed by pettifogging attorneys. They hire other men to fight because they have no loyalty, and abandon their liberty because they have no courage. We all know the process by which such a picture may be drawn of any people. If you test the waters of the purest stream, you may find places where it is full of corruption as the Thames; if you send out your spies to those social depressions into which the viler part of the population of any country drains, he may honestly bring back a report that he has seen none but blackguards. I hope, for the sake of this correspondent's veracity, and I believe from internal evidence, that he mixed exclusively with a society justly out of favour with their countrymen. To New York flows a very large share of the foreign and disloyal element of America. Wall-street is not more likely to take exalted patriotic views than our Stock Exchange; to judge of the American people by the gossip of a clique of Southern exiles, gold speculators, and refugee Irishmen in New York, is as absurd as it would have been to judge of the French Revolution exclusively from a Royalist *emigré*, or of English politics in the last century from a clique of Jacobites.   I have said that I do not know how far the *Times* holds itself responsible for the opinions of its correspondent.   It cannot, however, evade the responsibility of having given to him leave to vent in its pages some five or six weekly columns of unmixed abuse.   It may be presumed to have considered them at least valuable contributions to our knowledge of the time, and tolerably fair pictures of what was taking place. It thought, that is, that a portrait of America, in which every virtue was scrupulously omitted, was not a gross caricature.

In a more important way these letters affected the *Times*— namely, that they were the raw material of which a large part of the *Times'* articles were manufactured, and that their statements eked out a good many hints left judiciously vague in the leading articles.   To the popular mind the *Times* is hedged about with a certain mysterious divinity ; it is thought to be at any rate in possession of unusual sources of information.   A weight is attributed to its words which we should not give to the individual utterances of one of its writers.   A little steady reading of the *Times* will dissipate this idea.   The real process is this :   The New York correspondent hears that in some remote village some one has been tarred and feathered for Southern sympathies.   He ekes out half a column by telling this story at full length, which he can do with the more ease as the last military news was a Northern success, and will bear, like the battle of Gettysburg, to be dealt with in a few lines.   The *Times* writes upon this story ; or, to quit the abstraction for a moment, the *Times'* editor tells a contributor to send him an article upon it.   As the story is not a very long one, and even a *Times* article must come to the point after a certain number of flourishes, the column requires to be filled out.   The contributor, therefore, proves that the North have lost their liberties, and are passing through anarchy to despotism, and expands this sentiment by the help of a few of the absurd historical analogies which are always kept on hand. Thus a riot, equivalent perhaps to that which happened a few days ago at Nottingham*, is the nucleus of a formal sermon from the *Times* to prove that the American Government is in the hands of the mob. And most people, who have not been behind the scenes of a newspaper, incline to believe it, and suppose the opinion to rest upon profound observation of a political philosopher. The result is flimsy enough ; but as it is well understood that a *Times* article is subject to the careful supervision of the editor, we may assume that however slight the evidence may be, the editor believes that the North are in fact falling under despotic power with a force of conviction great enough to induce him to assert it in the most positive terms. How great that is, I can't say. It would, however, be desirable that people should understand that, as the strength of a chain is measured by its weakest link, so the broadest assertions of the *Times* about America frequently mean no more than rumour caught up by a silly *gobemouche* in the streets of New York.

IX.—A MILITARY DESPOTISM.

The educated and intelligent men who wrote in the *Times* could not but be aware that most historical events have causes. Unable to assign that which first presented itself, they were obliged to cast about for another. The hostile attitude to the Northern side, into which the *Times* had drifted so soon as the Northern side became, in its opinion, hopeless, made it extremely unwilling to admit the most obvious truths in regard to slavery. It took refuge in vehement assertions that the difference between North and South was as profound as the

* Since writing this I have seen this riot noticed in a French paper as a proof that Englishmen do not possess their boasted freedom of election.

difference between French and English, between Magyars and Germans, or between Germans and Italians; but it never condescended to specify in detail the nature of this profound difference; it could not, in fact, have done so without meeting its bugbear of slavery immediately beneath, if not actually upon, the surface. I have shown the prevarication and web of incessant self-contradiction into which the *Times* fell in accounting for the war; I have shown further that it led to a total misconception of the effect of the war upon slavery. I now have to show how the same embarrassment distorted its whole account of the machinery by which the war was carried on. The *Times* ignored any justification derivable from the circumstance that the aim and end of the struggle was the subversion of the slave power; it was driven to maintain that the case might be fairly paralleled in gratuitous wickedness with an attempt of France to conquer Holland. Moreover, it was as hopeless as an attempt of England to conquer France. A nation could have no rational motive for pursuing an enterprise proved by the *Times* to be at once wicked and hopeless. Two or three explanations of the phenomenon were possible. The nation might be mad, a theory much used by Sir A. Alison in explaining the French Revolution. Thus the *Times* (October 20, 1863) was inclined to agree with Bishop Berkeley that nations might go mad, like individuals. It was, however, too absurd for daily wear: it occurs in a few isolated expressions, which probably mean nothing more than that men who differ from the *Times* should, in charity, be held to be mad. Again, the war might be explained if it could be made out that by some mysterious process every one made it pay. On this supposition war would be enough to account for itself, and the *Times* be relieved of the necessity of any explanation; or, finally, it was conceivable that the people did not really care about the war, but were compelled to fight in obedience to some external will. This supposed the Government to be a despotism. In short, the Americans were either mad, mercenary, or slaves.

This last may be taken as the favourite theory of the *Times ;* and, as there were not wanting circumstances to give it a certain plausibility, I will state what I conceive to have been their real relation to the facts. That the development of great standing armies is dangerous to the liberties of a country, and that Republics are apt to be converted into Despotisms by successful military commanders, have become traditionary commonplaces. They have probably about as much value as such commonplaces usually possess, not, I should say, a very great one ; but, at any rate, they are frequently applied rashly and in accordance with a very strained and superficial analogy. In the great outburst in the United States, it might not unreasonably be supposed that constitutional changes might take place, that the distribution of power might be altered, and that a good deal of the old machinery might require repair, or give way under the strain. It is undeniable that in the Southern States, partially or wholly overrun by the Union forces, there existed for the time a military despotism, resting upon martial law—that is, upon the absence of all law—and often administered by vulgar governors, who frequently confounded brutality with energy. Again, in the Northern States it was an essential condition of the struggle that Government should be entrusted with great powers. Spies and sympathisers with the insurrection swarmed in the Northern cities. It was the boast of the South during the early part of the war that the plans of the Northern generals were invariably betrayed. In the attempted burning of Northern cities and in the assassination of Mr. Lincoln, we have had sufficient proof of the abundance of conspirators. Assuming that the war was to be carried on, it would have been childish to refuse the necessary powers to those who directed it. To relax the reins may be proof either that you cannot grasp them or that you are confident

that you can at any time resume them. The Government of the
United States are in theory the servants and the creatures of
the people.   In proportion as they are, in fact, dependent upon
the popular will, it is safe to entrust them for an emergency with
unrestricted authority, and when such authority has been
committed, it is absurd to quibble about its exercise in particular
instances.   When the ship is in extreme danger, the crew cannot
quarrel as to whether any officer has exceeded his duty.   Cases
of extreme individual hardship will in all probability occur; their
frequent occurrence would be a proof of bad management on the
part of the Government; a note should be made of them for
future redress, if immediate redress is impracticable ; but it would
be silly to make pretexts of them for depriving the Government of
its necessary discretionary power.

Now the whole question about the United States is whether
the powers exercised came under the class thus defined, or
whether they constituted a permanent encroachment upon
popular rights.   It will be at once admitted that the Constitution has undergone whatever change is implied in the
establishment by military force of the doctrine that the United
States form, as Webster maintained, a nation, and not, as
Calhoun maintained, a mere Confederacy resting on a compact.
It may be admitted further that the central power has been
strengthened and consolidated by the course of events.   But
we should be slow to admit, without distinct proof, that a
nation of some twenty millions of English-speaking inhabitants, brought up beyond all nations of the world in the habit
of settling their own affairs, and with an extraordinary aptitude
for expressing and enforcing the will of the majority, would
suffer this power to be snatched from their hands ; that a people
with whom newspapers seem to be a spontaneous product of the
soil of every village should allow the liberty of the press to be
tampered with except as a figure of speech ; or that a nation

distinguished for its almost exaggerated tendency to local self-government should allow its "liberties to be lost," as a man loses his pocket-handkerchief in a crowd. Stump orators might declaim about the *habeas corpus*, as during our own wars Sir F. Burdett talked about Magna Charta, or as, before his days, John Wilkes made orations about the British jury. But as Englishmen knew in those days that claptrap about loss of liberty was nothing but claptrap, Americans knew in our time that Mr. Benjamin Wood (whom the *Times* persistently mistook for a statesman) was as arrant a demagogue as John Wilkes, and talked as great nonsense. They were perfectly conscious that the war continued because an overwhelming majority wished it to continue; and that it was wiser to submit to occasional stretches of power than to be squabbling in the face of the enemy as to the exact amount of power to be doled out to their leaders;—wiser, because they were also conscious that they could resume the powers they had bestowed.

To quote language more forcible than my own, that namely of the *Times* itself—(Sept. 3, 1864)—"There is after all no " despotism possible in America, except the will of the majority." Lincoln and Seward only had power "because the mass of the " people really believed in the war and were anxious that their " leaders should carry things with a high hand." I may, perhaps, assume that if any despotism had been established, it was not, in September last, visible to the naked eye.

I will now quote a few previous utterances of the *Times* upon this subject; and I will point out the singular theory which they constructed. I must also quote some of the remarks of their New York correspondent, by which it was supplemented and enforced. That gentleman was, in fact, almost crazy about the loss of liberty. I should say, at a guess, that at least half of his whole correspondence was devoted to proving this loss by argument and illustrative stories; and, as his friends belonged to the class

most obnoxious to the United States Government, he was never at
a loss for legends of Fort Lafayette.   Of their accuracy, I have no
means of judging, but I should not be inclined to accept without
examination all the scandals which a Tory in 1776 might have told
us about Washington ; and it is conceivable that Mr. Seward
might correct some of the anecdotes that appear in the
Times.

The form of this " loss of liberty " which first appeared was the
expected advent of a Napoleon or a Cromwell.   (July 24, 1861.)
—The *Times* already augured that a volunteer force was becoming
a standing army, and as such, " dangerous to liberty."

Aug. 12, 1861.—It announced that a military dictator was not
improbable before twelve months were over ; the first definite
appearance of this mythical individual.   A candidate for the post
soon appeared in the character of General M'Clellan.

Jan. 29, 1862.—It informed us that " the clank of the sabre
" was already heard in the halls of the Legislature."   " The
" Federals already feel the weight of an armed hand upon
" themselves."

M'Clellan no more attempted to supplant the President than
the Duke of Wellington to make himself Emperor of the British
Isles.   The *Times'* correspondent, indeed, asserted (Oct. 7, 1862)
that " he (M'Clellan) held the twenty millions of the North in the
" palm of his hand," and that, " if he thought proper to depose
" the President, or let fall some such words as ' Take that bauble
" away,' his army would stand by him to the last man."

M'Clellan was soon afterwards dismissed as quietly as a light-
house-keeper.   The *Times* was utterly amazed, and even, as it
seems, annoyed at his forbearance.

" While M'Clellan," it says (November 24, 1862), " is in his
" camp with his army, surrounded by his friends, late one night a
" missive is put into his hands from a President who seems to
" have lost all influence, and from a Government which is

" gradually sinking into contempt, and immediately this powerful
" general lays down his command, sinks into a private individual,"
&c. . . . " Is it heroic patriotism or disgust, or the absence
" of ambition, or want of pluck, or is it policy?" It could not be
that the American people were not at the mercy of any military
adventurer, for, says the *Times*, " M'Clellan obeys the law, and he
" appears to be the only man in America who holds the law to be
" of any force."

This was a grievous disappointment. Moreover, no other
general for a long time acquired a sufficiently prominent position
to do the Napoleon trick. Even Grant, as we shall find out,
was beaten in almost every battle down to a certain day in the
spring of 1865. The *Times*, however, was convinced that the
place was ready: the man was all that was wanting. One or
two quotations will be sufficient from a multitude.

" Every republican form of government," as it asserted (Feb. 2,
1863), with a characteristic affectation of philosophy, "wherever
" found, has either gradually ripened and consolidated into a
" constitutional monarchy, or, which is the commoner result,
" violently merged into absolutism. There is nothing peculiar
" to America to arrest the milder process, except a headlong leap
" into the worse."

March 19, 1863.—In another pseudo-philosophical argument
ít asserts, after a deal of fine writing, that the Government at
Washington are now labouring " not to restore the Union "
(they might as well restore the Heptarchy), " but to reconquer
" what is lost, and let the worst come to the worst, to esta-
" blish a military power," or, as its correspondent assured it
(April 10, 1863)—for his piercing gaze was always discovering
things not yet revealed to the Americans themselves—there are
" many symptoms that this military dictatorship is not so remote a
" contingency as an easy public supposes. . . . The military
" machine is already constructed ; it only waits for the hardy

" engineer; the liberty of Federal America will be a tale that
" is told."

By May 27 the despotism was in existence, for " should peace
" be established," we are told, " the question would remain to be
" tried whether the Government of the United States should
" permanently become, what it undoubtedly now is, a military
" despotism," America being, it appears, " about to offer the
" last vestige of her liberties at the shrine of that Moloch of
" slaughter and devastation " (a playful term for Mr. Lincoln),
" which they have set up to reign over them."

The same gentleman had perhaps put this in the pithiest form
(Sept. 22, 1862) : " Were there half a Cromwell or a quarter
" of a Bonaparte, this overthrow " (of the Government) " would
" be the easy result of a *coup d'état.*"

It is curious after this to find the *Times* saying, in the autumn
of 1864, that a despotism is impossible in America.   It still, however, clung to the idea.   The Southern correspondent furnished
us with a sketch of Sherman's character for the express reason
that he was not unlikely to become the Cromwell of the future.

When Mr. Lincoln died, the *Times* expressed a hope that
Mr. Johnson might in some way be induced to resign.   " The
influences," it said (April 19), " by which he is surrounded cannot
" be favourable to his retention of office.   Grant and Sherman are
" both in or near Washington," and neither they nor Stanton
can wish to see their labours thrown away.

This hint was thrown away.   Sherman, having exceeded his
orders, instantly obeyed, as he could not but obey, the authority
of the President, and General Grant has shown no more signs of
being a Cromwell than did M'Clellan.   In short, strongly as the
Times seems to have expected, and even desired, the advent of a
military dictator, the military dictator never made his appearance.

The despotism, however, against which the *Times* most steadily
inveighed was that of Mr. Lincoln and his Cabinet.   I could

not, without doubling the size of this pamphlet, give any
adequate impression of the virulence, persistence, and energy
with which it repeated the assertion that Lincoln was a despot.
It seemed to cling to this as the one possible explanation of the
war. I will quote a few specimens, but they no more give an
idea of the whole than a bucketful of water gives an idea of a
lake. Incessant allusions to the loss of liberty fill up all the
spaces—often large enough—between their arguments, and show,
if my views are just, the curious distortion of their opinions.
They mistook a temporary and collateral effect of the war for
a real cause ; and because the North entrusted full powers to
their servants, fancied that the servants were the masters, and
a slavish compliance with their wishes the real incitement of
the war.

Sept. 12, 1861.—The *Times* "says nothing" of the sacrifice of
free institutions, the surrender of individual liberty, the establishment of the futile precautions of a despotism, the abolition of the
habeas corpus, the suppression of papers, the imprisonment of ladies,
and certainly nothing of gentlemen being ridden out of town on
a rail.

Sept. 6, 1862.—" Is a nation wise which embraces ruin and
" slaughter for the present in order to consolidate a government of
" terror and repression for the future ? Domiciliary visits and
" midnight arrests, without crime and without an accuser, are
" present to every one's mind."

Sept. 16.—" There is not one-tenth part of the liberty of
" opinion and discussion in America which exists in Republican
" France."

Oct. 28.—" To be suspect of being suspect is good cause for
" incarceration in North America. . . If the Republicans win
" (the elections), the war will go on for some time longer under
" the protection of a reign of terror."

They entertain some hopes, however, for (November 8, 1862)

they cannot but expect a democratic victory, as "a brilliant
" despotism may blind a nation for a time, but a Government
" that is at once stupid and tyrannical cannot long avert its own
" overthrow."

June 18, 1863.—The conscription was the one thing wanting to
make the Government a centralized military despotism. "The
" State organization will be dissolved. The Federal organization
" of the Republic will be destroyed. Bare and naked force will
" be set up as the only title to obedience and the only symbol of
" command."

Aug. 3.—Absolute power is probable. The issue (as between the Government and Vallandigham) is an issue between
liberty and despotism. "Whatever the President wills is law."
" The interests of the North are almost identical with those of the
" South ;" " both are in danger of subjugation at the hands of a
" third power,"—namely, the Federal Government.

Aug. 28.—The Constitution is being "rapidly moulded into
" a form which will make them in practice the greatest military
" despotism that the world has ever seen."

Nov. 28.—The main object of thanksgiving (Mr. Lincoln having
absurdly supposed that the victories of Gettysburg, Vicksburg, and
others, in the summer of 1863, deserved thanksgiving) should be
that, in such hands as Lincoln's, the State has hitherto escaped
total destruction. "Personal liberty is gone ; the Government
" rules by virtue of the army, which, unable to conquer the
" South, has an easy triumph over the laws and liberties of the
" North. We admit the Government to be, for the moment,
" strong, but refuse to believe that its strength is the result of that
" individual freedom which it has been its principal occupation to
" destroy."

May 11, 1864.—"The only freemen now are those that fight in
the war, or make their fortunes out of it."

Nov. 16.—Martial law has been declared wherever there is

a force sufficient to control the elections. " Every scholar has " wondered at the fatal rapidity with which the Roman Republic " ripened or rotted into an empire; but this is, in sober fact, the " process we now see across the Atlantic."

Nov. 22.—" We can regard his (Lincoln's) reappointment as " little less than the abdication by the American people of the " right of self-government, as an avowed step towards the founda- " tion of a military despotism; towards the suppression of a " popular Government which may still exist in form, but which, in " substance, has gone. Future historians will probably date from " the second presidency of Mr. Lincoln, the period when the " American Constitution was thoroughly abrogated, and had " entered on that transition state, well known to the students of " history, through which republics pass on their way from demo- " cracy to tyranny."

Feb. 28, 1865.—" Republican institutions are rapidly becoming imperial in almost all but the name."

If any reliance can be placed upon the *Times*, a consolidated military depotism now exists, and has for some time existed, in America. It has indeed this strange peculiarity, that, except in the suspension of the *habeas corpus* and the various arbitrary imprisonments which have been the consequence, it has committed no overt acts. The Constitutions of the several States remain in force, and are daily working much as before; the Constitution of the United States is unaltered, except by an impending amendment for the abolition of slavery. It is true, as I have before remarked, that one theory of the relations of the Central to the State Powers has been set up by force of arms; but it is a theory held at all times by many of the best American statesmen, and in no way incompatible with liberty. If the foul demon of despotism has indeed entered into the body of a free people, it must be admitted that that body, to external observation, moves about and has its being very much

as it had of old. Surely it is incumbent upon those who make
such reckless assertions to adduce some proof of their accuracy,
to point to some undeniable symptoms of the terrible disease
which is secretly corrupting the Constitution. The line between
liberty and despotism is not, as Englishmen ought to know, so
fine and impalpable that it requires wire-drawn argumentation
and delicate analytical processes to discover whether a country is
free or enslaved. When Cromwell or Napoleon had seized the
supreme authority it was felt, and heard, and seen; there was no
room for doubt upon the subject; there was no doubt about it, I
may add, when Butler governed New Orleans. At every turn
you were met by the unmistakable strong arm of military force
It wants no more argument to prove that a negro is a slave than
that he has woolly hair and blubber lips. Now the North are
conscious that they are free, and that the war was carried on
because and so long as they chose that it should be carried on.
The small minority who objected had necessarily to suffer the
unpleasant fate of seeing their country fighting in what they
believed to be a wrong and foolish quarrel. Individuals might
for the time suffer from the authority necessarily entrusted to
rulers, and, doubtless, often foolishly exercised; but, now that
the war is over, even the *Times* will hardly dare to assert that the
North are not a free people. Indeed, the shallowness of its
conviction to the contrary is strikingly proved by the passage I
have quoted from September 3, 1864, that " there is no despotism
possible in America." Had the despotism existed except as a
mere figment of its imagination preserved in fictitious vitality
as a useful taunt, such an assertion at such a time would have
been impossible; it would have been as hard as for a doctor to
assert that a patient in the last stage of a consumption, when he
had been for many months under his treatment, had perfectly
sound lungs, so sound as to be incapable of disease. If the
burden of proof were thrown upon me, I could point to the

disbandment of armies as unlike a military despotism—to the immediate and almost precipitate effort at "reconstruction" as hardly like a complete oblivion of popular government; I might point to a free press, which, even during the heat of the war, when the administration was strongest, incessantly attacked it with a bitterness rivalling the bitterness of the *Times*, and which would have been permitted in no country on the continent of Europe; and to the constant discussion and decision of every political principle by the people in every corner of the land. But I don't wish to spend time upon proving that the sun shines; I must endeavour to show how the *Times* endeavoured to make out that all the external appearances of self-government were in reality delusive; that whilst the patient seemed to be walking and talking as freely as a man well could who had so tremendous a task to perform, he was really gagged and tied hand and foot.

If a despotism "in any other sense," as the *Times* says, " than a despotism of the majority," should ever be forced upon America, it would have two tasks to perform. It would have to corrupt the elections, and it would have to support itself by an army alien in sympathy from the people. Under these conditions a Government might be set up which did not fairly represent the popular will, and might be maintained in defiance of it.

The *Times* made, as I will now show, an attempt to prove that each of these methods had been adopted.

X.—THE INSTRUMENTS OF . DESPOTISM.

Although, as I have said, the *Times* occasionally threw out hints, rather than positive assertions, that the elections were fictitious and enforced under military error, this opinion was so slightly founded on fact (I speak, of course, of the Northern States) as to be generally left to the New York correspondent. His occasional statements, coinciding with general declamations in the *Times* leaders about "military despotism," tended to com-

plete the picture; but I do not find that the *Times* often gave
them the weight of its own authority.   I will give a couple of
instances.   The elections in the autumn of 1863 were of considerable interest, and gave large majorities to the Republicans.
Vallandigham was the candidate for Governor in Ohio.

March 11, 1863.—The correspondent asserted that the Republican party, always a minority and now desperate, were endeavouring to subjugate their own countrymen.   The Conscription
Act was intended to supply a force to hold down the States
during the approaching election for the Presidency.   The conscripts of each State will be sent to do duty in States with the
people of which they have no sympathy.   (October 13.)—He
announced that Vallandigham's election was to be prevented,
if necessary, by getting up disturbances and then proclaiming
martial law.

I need not say that martial law was not declared nor Vallandigham elected.   At this time the "special correspondent," whom
I have already mentioned, was in the United States and present at
Cincinnati.   Although unfriendly on the whole to the Northern
cause, he says positively (October 31) there were but a dozen or a
score of policemen at each polling-place.   The public authorities
nowhere interfered.   " I saw soldiers nowhere, Irish bullies
" nowhere, nowhere an attempt—I will not say to force—but
" even to solicit a vote."

Meanwhile, the New York correspondent was writing (Oct. 30)
vague assertions about greenbacks, and the threats of provost-
marshals.   It was well that this time he had a brother correspondent actually on the spot to contradict him flatly.

The most important election was that at which Mr. Lincoln was
elected for the second time.   The *Times* asserted (November 16,
1864), that martial law had been proclaimed wherever there was a
force sufficient to control the elections.   After the elections—that
is, after receiving the news of the election—the *Times* never ven-

tured for a moment to repeat this assertion. Indeed, it is expressly admitted (December 31, 1864), that Mr. Lincoln was the *bonâ fide* choice of the nation.

One curious circumstance about the election was, that the New York correspondent made an apology for a misstatement, the only instance that I have found of his so doing, and confessed unreservedly (January 9, 1865) that he had been mistaken in asserting that General Dix had ordered military occupation of polling-places on the frontier. The fact was, as he admitted, that General Dix had occupied certain posts to guard against raids from Canada, but had withdrawn the forces before the day of the election. One more remark may be added on this subject. The *Times* had, for a long time, looked upon the Chicago platform, that upon which General M'Clellan was nominated, as a proof of a return of Americans to reasonable—that is, to peace—principles. So strongly did it hold this, that it (September 14, 1864) compared some of Sherman's battles near Atlanta to the Battle of Toulouse, fought after peace was declared—a blunder into which it was, as usual, led by the confident assertions of its correspondent. The Democrats, whose principles were repre-sented on that platform, were a minority of the whole nation. Now (September 26, 1864) the *Times* confessed that this platform was a complete failure, because it was an attempt to combine war and peace Democrats; that is, the majority even of the Demo-cratic party were in favour of war, though of a war carried on upon different principles. As the Republicans were unanimously in favour of war, it follows that an overwhelming majority of the whole American people were, on the showing of the *Times* itself, in favour of continuing the war so late as the autumn of 1864. Hence the hypothesis that the war was the act of the Government, or, as the New York correspondent says, of a desperate minority forcing it upon their countrymen, becomes absurd. No one will probably now deny that the election of Mr. Lincoln expressed what was, however foolish, the settled decision of the American people.

The attempt to prove that the army was one suited for a despotic power was far more persistently carried on.   It was not, indeed, merely for this reason that we were so constantly informed that the Federal army consisted of Irish and Germans. It was an inviting topic of abuse for many reasons, and of all the misrepresentations that were so common, none, as I believe, not even that vast and complicated misrepresentation which ignored the relations of slavery to the war, did so much to excite English prejudices as this story about the Irish and Germans.   There is an ambiguity about this subject which must be shortly stated.   There were in America, by the census of 1860, over 4,000,000 inhabitants of foreign birth— including, Irish, 1,600,000 ; Germans, 1,300,000 ; and English and Scotch, 540,000—more than 3,500,000 of whom were in the North. Now these naturalized citizens, who had emigrated in the *bonâ fide* intention of settling in the United States before the first shot had been fired, were undoubtedly as much justified in fighting for the country of their adoption as the native Americans.   They might even be expected to enlist in greater proportion than the native population, because they would naturally furnish more of that floating class from which the armies of all countries are chiefly recruited.   The real accusation was, that the American armies were supplied by persons emigrating from Europe with a view to this very purpose.

In this case, again, the accusation is in one respect trivial enough.   It is a favourite taunt of the *Times* (see, for example, July 4, 1862, and May 21 and July 4, 1863), that whereas the Americans used to complain of our employment of Hessian troops in the War of Independence, they now use foreigners themselves.   This comes with a rather bad grace from a nation which raised a foreign legion so lately as in the Crimean war.

It implies a total misrepresentation of the true grounds of complaint. No one would have complained of our enlisting Germans, or Frenchmen, or any other foreigners in our regiments ; and, in fact, I presume that no questions were asked as to the nationality of a recruit. But that which covered the German princes with an infamy which we shared to some extent was, that they sold their regiments to us wholesale without asking their consent. If an Irishman likes to exchange potatoes in a Connaught cabin for the good fare and comfortable clothing of a Federal soldier balanced by the chance of being shot, he may or may not show want of sense, but there is no hardship in the case. If we had sold a regiment of Irishmen, or if the King of Prussia had sold a regiment of Germans, to either side, for money to be paid to the proprietor of the regiment, there would have been infamy enough. Happily we are too civilized for such transactions to be possible. The *Times* carefully ignored the distinction.

It would, however, be a proof that the American people were not enthusiastic about the war, and that a fit instrument of bondage was being framed for them, if it could be proved that the army was kept up by immigration, and not by recruits from the native population. The *Times* repeatedly asserted, or insinuated, that this was the case. I quote a few instances :—

So early as July 30, 1861, it speaks of "a standing army in which Germans and Irish are counted by the thousand."

July 26, 1862.—"The army is to a very great extent a foreign " army, being composed of German and Irish mercenaries ; and " the native Americans who have joined them belong to no very " respectable class."

Six weeks before this it had observed incidentally (June 4) that " every New England family has its representative in the field "— a statement which was strongly confirmed by the special corre- spondent a year after.

August 26, however, it tells us again that, as the conscription

will induce all foreigners to leave the States (we shall presently
see the fulfilment of the prognostication), "we shall now see
" American citizens fighting their own battles, without the aid of
" German and Irish mercenaries."

Dec. 30.—"Their men are for the most part mere hirelings;
" the refuse of Ireland and Germany has been swept into their
" camps at so many dollars a head."

June 18, 1863.—It speaks of the willingness of the Americans
to undergo all extremities, "so long as the physical suffering is
" borne by Irish and Germans, and the pecuniary by the public
" creditor."

July 4.—The United States Government are "sending to
" indiscriminate slaughter myriads of German and Irish mer-
" cenaries."

Aug. 8.—What does the Washington Cabinet care " how many
" graves are dug round Fort Wagner or how many regiments of
" Irish and German emigrants monthly disappear ?"

Before continuing my quotations from the *Times* I will give
one or two passages from the New York correspondent. This
question placed that gentleman in a curious dilemma. He was
constantly endeavouring to prove that it would be impossible to
raise an army, and that, for various reasons, no more Germans or
Irish would volunteer. On the other hand, he was always proving
that the whole army was composed of Germans and Irishmen.
The result is sometimes perplexing, and appears to have bewildered
his employers. Prospectively, no Germans nor Irish were to be
found ; retrospectively, the army consisted of nothing else. It
was indeed impossible to understand how, upon his showing, it
was kept up at all.

June 30, 1862.—He tells us that the Yankees have con
tributed little to the rank and file of the Federal army ; Irish and
Germans form at least two-fifths of the whole number of fighting
men.

July 27 —With amusing precision, he says, to show the absence of loyalty, that the North can only obtain thirty-nine seamen from all the New England States.

Sept. 16.—It appears that the armies are kept up by wretched emigrants drugged with whisky, who " wake up only to find " themselves in the Northern camp, liable if they skedaddle to " be shot as deserters."

Feb. 21, 1863.—We have another careful numerical calculation proving that there are only 32,330 able-bodied negroes in the free States, that as the Government won't dare to recruit in the border States, and can't get at the South, negro troops enough can never be raised. (Fifteen months afterwards, May 12, 1864, he tells us that there are 130,000 negroes in the service, 97,670 having, I presume, been manufactured.)

June 15.—He proves that it is impossible to raise 10,000 negroes.

I have taken these specimens at random from an immense number as indicating the general tone of the New York correspondent. He generally maintains that negroes can't be got, that Yankees won't volunteer, and that the armies are composed of Irish and Germans, though, as we shall now see, he frequently states that Irish and Germans are equally recusant. The continual existence of the army seems to be all but miraculous. Up to this point, however, the *Times* and its correspondent agree in asserting the absence of native material from the United States army, and agree in filling the void by any number of Germans and Irish.

Aug. 25, 1863.—The *Times* made the calculation, an extremely rough one, that 750,000 men had been killed or put *hors de combat* up to that time on the two sides. And as it allowed 500,000 of these to the North, it came to the conclusion that the " bulk of the Germans and Irish complained of by the South must have been naturalized American citizens "— a tolerably reasonable conclusion, though founded upon doubtful figures and contradicting its own repeated insinuations.

Oct. 9.—The correspondent, however, informs us that " the " zeal of the native-born Americans has died away, the unwelcome " business is left to raw new comers from Germany and Ireland " —a statement which brings back our old friends again.

Perhaps the assertion that the army was composed of foreign elements might be gradually coming true, though it had not been true at first. The original troops may have been native, the recruits foreign.

Dec. 12.—He explains again that the army could not be kept up were it not for the Irish and German immigrants and negroes; the latter especially, he says, will constitute the sheet-anchor of the future American army. (Compare the quotations above from February 21 and June 15.)

Jan. 23, 1864.—He declares that no more men are to be got. The foreign immigration would only produce 156,000 men, even if all were able-bodied, whereas at least fifty per cent. were children, women, and old men ; three hundred thousand are required.

May 3, 1864.—However, the *Times* states that the waste of men is supported by immigration attracted by large bounties, and carefully explains how the " surplus population of Europe " is attracted.

April 18.—The correspondent says that the North would long ago have been subdued but for the help of foreigners, but that now the Irish and Germans are in a state of chronic discontent, and won't volunteer.

After all this, it is not a little surprising to find a demonstration in the *Times* itself, that the immigration theory is all a mistake. A debate took place in Parliament upon the Irish emigration. In commenting upon it, the *Times* says (June 11, 1864), that Grant alone has 280,000 white troops, that the Irish emigration of 1863 was 94,477, of whom 36,083 only were men, including boys of twelve years old. It concludes, " With such figures before " us, it is impossible to assume that either German or Irish " emigrants up to the present time form any large element in the " American armies. Eighty per cent. of these troops must have " been Americans, native or naturalized."

After this statement, it would be reasonable to suppose that the *Times* would apologize. But the *Times* never apologizes, it simply reverses its statements.

July 2.—It boldly declared that Grant's army was kept up by " an incredible immigration from Europe."

As the *Times* had so plainly proved that the immigration of 1863 was utterly inadequate to fill the ranks, I may remark that the immigration at New York (the principal port for immigration) only increased from 155,000 in 1863 to 185,000 in 1864,—an ample proof that this " incredible immigration " was a mere invention of the *Times*. It continued the old taunts.

Aug. 2.—" It is felt to be quite a pity not to go on with a war " the worst consumption of which can be supplied from the old " world."

The correspondent (August 13) throws some light upon the " incredible immigration." " The average volunteers," he tells us, " inclusive of Irish and Germans, scarcely exceed thirty a day." The more one looks into this warlike stream of immigrants, the harder it is to distinguish it. Finally, the *Times* itself came out with the most conclusive exposure of its own errors.

February 21, 1865.—After giving the numbers raised for the Federal army, it remarks with amusing complacency, " We have " repeatedly explained that immigration would only account for a " small fraction of these results. Even if every adult male " immigrant took service in the Federal army immediately upon " landing, the supply would only form a very moderate per- " centage on the levies raised," and it is notoriously true that

nothing of the kind took place.   There is something truly
surprising about this.   The *Daily News* or the *Star* might have
quoted the same statistics to prove the falsehood of the incessant
taunts of the *Times*.   The *Herald* or *Standard*, accepting as an
axiom that everything American is abominable, would in honest
bigotry have thrown doubt upon the figures or roundly denied
their accuracy.   It was peculiar to the *Times* to give at once the
calumny and its refutation with an air of unruffled dignity.*

The statement that the military despotism was supported by
mock elections in the Northern States may be considered as tacitly
abandoned.   Had any proofs been at hand capable of raising a
presumption that the very sources of self-government were thus
being poisoned, the *Times* might have been trusted to adduce
them.   We may, then, assume that, notwithstanding the existence
of the ordinary, or more than the ordinary, corruption, the
electors substantially expressed the will of the people.

The theory that the military despotism was upheld by a foreign
army is refuted, as well as asserted, by the *Times* itself.   The
notion that "conscripts from each State would be quartered in
States with which they had no sympathies" is an amusing instance
of the readiness of the New York correspondent to swallow the
most unfounded fictions.

One other theory remains—that the despotism corrupted the
people by greenbacks ; and on this, as it was a favourite opinion,
and one which, so far as I know, was never definitely abandoned,
I must say a few words.   I will quote one or two assertions from
the *Times*.

Feb. 3, 1862.—" It is pretty clear now that war is kept up by a
" fictitious public enthusiasm, founded upon squandering among

---

* I have not been able to find any official statement as to the extent of the
foreign element in the American armies : but it is said, on good authority, to
be about five per cent.; that of naturalized being fifteen per cent. ; and that of
native Americans eighty per cent. of the whole strength.

" the small class of political contractors and agitators two million
" dollars a day."

Jan. 20, 1863.—" The people have turned the war into a
" scramble for profits ; the army of public banditti have won a full
" and decisive victory in the field for gain."

June 18.—It seems that the war is carried on partly from
" reckless fanaticism," and partly " to glut the avarice of a few
obscure persons."

I need not quote any of the incessant assertions to the same
effect of the New York correspondent, who was never so happy
as when proving that Northern patriotism meant a lust for greenbacks, and Northern Abolitionism was a mixture of hypocrisy and
fanaticism.   The theory of the *Times* took a slightly different
form at a later period of the war.   It believed in the existence of
what it called a " fictitious prosperity," and was not a little per-
plexed to account for its extraordinary duration.   The bubble
would not burst long after the *Times* had declared that it
inevitably must.

Thus (Nov. 28, 1863) we are told that " the factitious creation
" of wealth by reckless issues of paper money, and the equally
" reckless reduction of the available amount of labour by fearful
" slaughter of the working classes in civil war, may raise the rate
" of wages, and so tempt to emigrate the inhabitants of populous
" countries.   These things give little hope for the future prospects
" of a country that really seems to verify the paradox of the
" poet, ' where (paper) wealth accumulates and men decay.'"

On December 14, 1863, it expresses its amazement at the
duration of a fictitious prosperity which an inflated currency and
a prodigal expenditure are sure to produce for the time.

I believe that on the strength of these and similar statements
many persons in England seriously believed that the war was
carried on because, by some strange commercial hocus-pocus,
it paid, or seemed to pay, for itself.   It was a kind of Law's

scheme, stimulated and accompanied by a war.   There are some
men who will always gladly believe that great results can be
accomplished by petty motives—men who would once have
delighted to explain the French Revolution by the gold of Pitt,
or the American war of independence by speculations in tea.
This explanation of the war would be congenial to them.
A great revolution worked out by inferior instruments, a tremendous convulsion of a society composed in overwhelming pro-
portions of half-educated and half-refined men, must infallibly
bring to the surface much that is shocking to delicate tastes.
There were chances of profit for the large class, nowhere larger
than in America, to whom even national honour would afford
mere matter of speculation.   In a struggle which shook society
to its base, there was good scrambling for high prizes.   But it is
scarcely characteristic of a generous or of a philosophical mind,
to mistake the profit incidentally arising to stock-jobbers and
shoddy manufacturers for the cause of the whole struggle.
Nations are moved to their depths, and efforts which would
strain the most unbounded resources are stimulated, by deeper
and less grovelling motives than the hope of picking up a few
dollars in the confusion.   A battle, doubtless, is a good thing
for the crows and the creeping things ; but it is not generally
fought for their benefit.   The theory, stated plainly, confutes
itself so conclusively that I need scarcely point out that its
political economy presents a few difficulties.   Perhaps this may
be due to the fact that, as the *Times* put it (June 24, 1862),
" the world is not large enough to hold " political economy
and the United States " together."   I can understand a
" fictitious prosperity " produced by borrowing other people's
money ; but the American debt was raised at home almost
entirely.   I can understand that " fictitious prosperity " which
accompanies a great inflation of credit, and a consequent increase
of circulation, and which lasts until persons have begun to realize.

But credit has not been inflated in the United States; the paper currency has produced its natural effect in the rise of prices; and so soon as that effect commenced, the Yankee was quite acute enough to discover that his paper dollar was worth less than his silver dollar. A fictitious prosperity of this kind lasting for four years is simply incredible. The fact that it has not long ago collapsed is proof enough that the prosperity, such as it was, was really due to great resources, not to imaginary wealth. The simple truth is, that turning capital from other industries into the production of divers machines for blowing men to bits, does not tend to make a country richer, or even to make it think itself richer for any length of time. Even the receipt of killing off a large proportion of the able-bodied males would not necessarily cause such a rise of wages as to add to the general prosperity of the country. Widows and orphans are apt to make their presence known.

Granting, however, that there was some truth caricatured in these statements, it is plain enough, from one simple consideration, that they do not reveal a true cause of the continuance of the war. The centres of the "shoddy" interest were the places most opposed to the policy of the Administration, such as the city of New York. That policy was most unflinchingly supported by the country districts of the "territorial democracy," where the drain of labour and the rise of prices were most severely felt, and to which the contractors' profits never penetrated.

XI.—MILITARY CRITICISM.

I have endeavoured to show that the *Times* gave a preposterous caricature of the origin of the war. of its effect upon the country, and of the means by which it was maintained. The prejudice, which denied the war to be in any way related to slavery, and which denied that it was leading to any result but a military

despotism, led to an equal distortion of the facts of the war. I
shall endeavour to illustrate this by giving a short summary of
the *Times*' account of the last year of the war. I may remark
that any one who believes in the impartiality of the *Times* would
do well to compare these articles with an extremely able series
which appeared in the *Globe*—a paper not favourable to the
North, but quite above the folly of distorting the facts of the
war.

The fortunes of the Confederacy culminated in the spring of
1863. In the East, General Lee was able to make his most
determined effort at an invasion of the North. In the West,
Grant was detained for months before Vicksburg, and a long
delay produced in the otherwise almost uniform progress of the
Federal arms in the Western States. The battle of Gettysburg
and the taking of Vicksburg, which occurred on the 4th of July,
marked the turn of the tide. In the autumn, Rosecrans cleared
Tennessee and advanced to Chattanooga. He was severely
defeated at Chickamauga, but the fortunes of the North were
restored by Grant's victory on Missionary Ridge. At the close
of 1863 the Northern side was distinctly in the ascendant. In
1864, as we all remember, Grant fought the desperate series of
battles which resulted in the siege of Petersburg. Sherman
forced his way to Atlanta and thence to the Atlantic coast. The
series of victories under which the Confederacy collapsed are
fresh in our memories. Let me now give the *Times*' account of
these events.

The *Times* (July 9, 1863) had explained, on Lee's invasion,
that there was a general wish throughout the North that President
Davis might instal himself at Washington. Even after the arrival
of the decisive news (July 18, 1863) it declared Meade to be in
danger and Grant in a hopeless position. (July 23.)—It could
still see no reason for the Northern exultation. (July 27.)—The
news being beyond question, it observed that "Lee had only

" been prevented by three days' bloody fighting from obtaining
" important military successes "—a circumlocution which may
compare with the ingenious formulæ about " strategic movements,"
and " drawing a man further from his base." The New York
riots, however, proved that "the hopelessness of the [Northern]
" enterprise is never more evident than at the time when it seems
" most promising." This consoling reflection was strengthened
by Morgan's raid into Ohio, which, it may be recollected, ended
in the capture of Morgan and all his men. In November,
Mr. Lincoln had the bad taste to call for a public thanksgiving.
The *Times* was astonished. " It is," it remarked, " simply
" absurd to say that the condition of the South is worse, rela-
" tively to the North, than it was at the beginning of the war."

It had been encouraged by Rosecrans' defeat at Chickamauga and temporary confinement at Chattanooga. Having
entirely forgotten the existence of Grant's army—part of which,
under Sherman, reinforced the army at Chattanooga with decisive
effect—it announced (November 10) that " Thomas's success "
(Thomas was then in command at Chattanooga) " depends upon
" his union with Burnside " (then at Knoxville) , " he cannot
" expect considerable reinforcements from any other quarter."
By " success," it explains that it means escape from surrender.
(November 14.)—It announces that "the best that can be expected
" from the invaders of Tennessee is to be spared a ruinous and
" ignominious retreat." The campaign of 1863 has ended
leaving matters in the same state as in the beginning. (November 23.)—The Northern forces in the West are in exactly the
same state as those of the English at Yorktown and Saratoga.
" It will be an extraordinary instance of good fortune if Grant is
able to rescue " Burnside. Grant defeated Bragg, as I have
observed, at Missionary Ridge. The *Times*, however, in summing
up results, observed (December 14) that the Federals had in this
year " gained the one real victory of the war. We can hardly

" describe by that name the success of Grant against Bragg, but
" Gettysburg was a pitched battle fairly won."

To explain this assertion about one of the most decided and
skilfully planned victories of the war, I must remark that the
Times, like its sporting contemporaries, kept a private prophet,
one " S." This gentleman was always prophesying with signal
want of success, as his prophecies were simply renewed appli-
cations of one single dogma, viz., that the more territory the
North conquered the more they would have to keep (which is
undeniable), and therefore the harder it would be to keep it
(which does not follow). This prophet had assured the *Times*
(on December 11) that Bragg was in the act of falling back
when Grant attacked him, that there was nothing in the nature
of a pitched battle, and that everything depended upon the
struggle at Knoxville. The *Times* apparently considered " S."
as a military critic of some skill, to judge from the space which
they assigned to his letters, and their frequent coincidence
with his opinions. The taking of Vicksburg was not to be
counted in the list of victories, I presume, because, as the *Times*
occasionally pointed out, the Confederates could command other
points on the Mississippi.

At the commencement of 1864 the North were therefore in a
bad way.

Feb. 17.—The North have only kept up their armies by the
help of negroes and foreigners. " Longstreet has been entirely
successful in his operations round Knoxville." (He did not take
it, but that, of course, is a trifle.) The Confederates have met
their enemy at every point. Hence, we are not surprised to
hear that (May 3) the "present prospects of the Confederates
at this fourth year of the war are brighter than ever."

The great operations of 1864 now began, Grant assaulting
the right and Sherman the left of the long Confederate line.
In both quarters the Confederates retired, in obedience to a

preconcerted plan. Thus (May 24) Lee's falling back was
" preconcerted." (June 3.)—" The latest news prepares us for
the complete failure of Grant's expedition." Johnson's retreat
before Sherman "may have been a preconcerted plan to draw
Sherman away from his base of operations." As for Grant,
it appeared presently (June 7) that "it is hard enough to get to
" Richmond; it will be still harder to discover when they [the
" Federals] get there what they have gained by the enterprise,
" which has cost them such enormous sacrifices." (June 8.)—
" We recognize the truth of President Davis's saying," that Virginia alone could hold out twenty years after the fall of Richmond.

Every successive move of Grant's was a failure. (July 2.)—
Every move in this campaign " has been made because the
former manœuvre failed." Lee " did not deign to interrupt
Grant's flank march." Grant persevered, or, as the *Times* put
it (August 31), " still hovered about Richmond." Some relief
to the dismal prospect was given by Sheridan's victory in the
Shenandoah Valley; but this (October 3) was of more
importance politically than in a military sense. Sheridan's
success must have been valueless; for, as the *Times* observes
(December 2), Sherman's taking of Atlanta is the chief Federal
achievement of the year, and that is likely to end in disaster.

Sept. 15.—Grant's campaign had, as " S." assured them, " so
" completely broken down as almost to have passed from
" attention," as in fact might be expected from a previous
assertion of " S." that " Grant was as much a general as Tom
Sayers " (June 6); M'Clellan having "shown clearly enough
the way to take Richmond," whereas Grant, " with a rare
obliquity of judgment," had taken "a road difficult beyond all
others, and through country special unpromising." "S." doubtless
knew Grant's and M'Clellan's business better than Grant and
M'Clellan themselves, for he had pooh-poohed the former pretender
to military science in almost the same terms. " M'Clellan," he

said (May 5, 1862), "has taken the worst possible means of advancing on Richmond." In obedience to this great authority, the *Times* asserted (November 7, 1864) the "one principle of Federal warfare" to be to give away two Federals, five Federals, ten Federals for a "single Confederate life," and Grant blundered on from failure to failure, unconscious, it must be hoped, that he was acting in defiance of the *Times* criticisms.

Meanwhile, Sherman was being drawn farther from his base. (July 7.)—If Grant were repulsed, Sherman must be overwhelmed. Sherman managed to struggle on, and at last threatened Atlanta. The *Times* announced (August 8) that Atlanta was in danger. The value of the · success was measurable by the assertion that the capture of the arsenal might compensate the North for the invasion of Maryland. Sherman, however, was in serious danger, which became gradually more alarming. (September 12.) —He has managed to get into Atlanta, but will probably be cut off. Although (September 20) his campaign contrasts favourably with Grant's, the value of the prize is doubtful. Indeed (September 22) it is proved to be almost valueless by the fact that he did not attack the enemy's intrenchments only six miles off. His danger became gradually imminent. Atlanta (November 10) was really of no importance. Indeed (November 12), "the " barren victory in the Shenandoah Valley was all the Federals " had to boast of in the autumn," for Sherman's position was rapidly becoming untenable. (December 2.)—As I have before observed, it appears that Sherman's capture of Atlanta was the chief Federal success of the year, and that if Sherman should be finally beaten the balance would be against the Federals. For Sherman was already in "retreat" once more. (December 3.)— Sherman, we are told, had reached Atlanta, but there his triumphs ended. Hood speedily made the place untenable.

It scarcely admitted of a doubt that Sherman's expedition must result in a disaster. Everything looked unfavourable. "The most

" remarkable feature of the war," it says (December 22), " is the
" wild and desperate effort of an out-manœuvred general to
" extricate himself from his position." At length news came,
filtered through Southern sources, and worked up by the *Times*
into one of the most curious masses of error to be found even in
its pages. (December 26, 1864.)—It announced that Sherman
was emerging. His object was to reach the sea at any price. He
had with him " only half the force he took from Atlanta." (This
was a misrepresentation, apparently, of a statement that half
Sherman's army had at some part of the march been sent to
threaten Augusta.) " The Savannah was navigable for 400 miles
above the point at which Sherman is approaching it." (It is
navigable for 250 in all.) The Ogeechee is one of the tributaries
of the Savannah. (The Savannah and Ogeechee flow parallel
to each other, and guarded Sherman's two flanks; the *Times*
forced the Ogeechee into the Savannah, with the apparent
intention of cutting off Sherman's " retreat.") Sherman could
have no serious intention of taking Savannah. It is supposed
that he intends to cross the Savannah to meet a force sent east
wards from Port Royal to meet him. This force was, no doubt,
assumed to be so mystified by the sudden changes in geography as
to move in precisely the opposite direction to that which in a
normal state of things would bring it to meet Sherman.

Besides these main armies, General Banks had made an expedition from New Orleans, and completely failed. As the Confederates
began the year with brighter prospects than ever before, as Grant
lost battle after battle at a fabulous cost of life, as Sherman was
retreating with little hope of safety, and Banks had been all but
crushed, it is not surprising that the *Times* continued to think the
Northern cause hopeless. Suddenly the ground it had thought so
solid gave way under its feet. Savannah surrendered, Wilmington
was taken, Charleston was taken, and Sherman pierced South
Carolina as he had pierced Georgia. The Confederacy seemed to

be that hollow shell to which Mr. Seward had compared it, much
to the amusement of the *Times*. For a time it made a feeble
attempt at maintaining that, after all, the loss was not so great.
The "first act" of the war was over. But that only had happened
which "all Europe" had expected to happen at once, and if the
South stood firm the end was no nearer. A guerilla warfare
might be expected to succeed to the conflicts of regular armies.
Suddenly Grant defeated Lee, and with the capture of Richmond the war practically expired. The *Times'* correspondent still
remained faithful. He hinted even (April 18) that the conclusive
victory was rather " theatrical " than substantial, and that Lee
was retreating when it took place on a preconcerted plan. The last
flutter of this gentleman, as I may here mention, was an attempt
to prove that Texas might still hold out for years ; the letter was
written after the last Texas general had surrendered. The *Times*
had but one excuse, and that an absurdly feeble excuse, to make.
The whole fortune of the war, it said (April 17), had been
changed by the errors of the generals opposed to Sherman. If
President Davis had not superseded Johnson, things might have
gone differently.

The "ifs" of history are innumerable ; but this can hardly be
a serious statement. Every item of news from the South makes
the truth more evident. Impartial observers had remarked it
during the war, but the *Times* had refused to see it. The
simple fact is, that of two gamblers who stake equal amounts
with widely different fortunes, the poorer will be ruined first.
The last reserves win the battle. The Southern cause was
bleeding to death whilst the North had hardly developed its
full strength. There were abundant symptoms of the fatal
weakness, but the *Times* apparently put faith in its New York
correspondent (a degree of credulity of which one would have
thought the *Times* specially unlikely to be guilty), and supposed
these statements to be mere Northern forgeries. The *Times*, in

fact, by a curious mental hallucination, appeared to think that the Southern soldiers were immortal. When it calculated that Lee had only been prevented from winning a great success by three days' hard fighting, it never occurred to the writer that this failure of success was necessarily a tremendous loss, and that even a Southern victory might easily be bought too dear. The losses of the North were constantly kept before the English imagination by the incessant calculations and exaggerations of the New York correspondent. The Southern losses were carefully concealed, and the Confederacy presented for a long time an apparently unbroken front. But any one whose thoughts were too deep, must have known that the loss was not the less severe because not openly avowed.

There is one more remark to be made. The failure to take into account the element of slavery still misled the *Times'* judgment. It said (Nov. 7, 1864) that the negro would fight for his master. As the experiment was not tried, it is impossible to say whether this is true ; but it is at least significant that the masters did not venture to try the experiment until the last extremity. The employment of blacks by the Federal troops had a very different effect from that which would have followed their employment by the Confederates. It is clear gain if you can make a battering-ram against your enemy's fort of a beam taken from his own foundations. It is by no means gain to him to use the same material for an opposing machine. However this may be, slavery produced one cardinal weakness in the Southern defences which the *Times* was forced studiously to ignore. Wherever the Federal forces went they stayed. They found half the population at least passively friendly, and by freeing them, they, for the time, paralyzed the hostile moiety. But the *Times*, by averting its sight from all that concerned emancipation, except where emancipation involved accidental cruelty, failed to allow for this in its calculations.

XII.—MORAL.

On Dec. 31, 1863, after speaking of the "foolish vituperation of England" which had been fashionable with the American press, the *Times* added, with superlative calmness, "the entire absence of "retaliation on the English side can scarcely be claimed as a "merit; the spectator is naturally calmer than the combatant, "nor is he tempted to echo his incoherent cries."

This remark suggests a few rather curious reflections. The American press is accused of "foolish vituperation of England." I fully concur in the justice of this charge. From the *New York Herald* upwards there is much which no Englishman can read— few Englishmen, happily, read it at all—without a certain jar upon his patriotic sensibilities. The truth is that human nature on both sides of the Atlantic is tolerably alike, and that in both countries angry men use strong language, and men in the excitement of a life-and-death struggle don't pause to adjust their epithets or qualify their judgments with nicety. This is indeed admitted by the writer in the *Times.* He might with perfect fairness have gone further. The American press has, from the nature of the case, no such concentration of able and scholarlike writers as those of our metropolitan and best provincial papers. It is far inferior to ours in talent. I cannot so well judge as to its principles; but I am inclined to believe that we should find it impossible to produce any match for the *New York Herald* in thorough baseness and disposition to pander to the worst popular tastes. On the other hand, they have many journals, which appear to me to be as honestly but not so ably conducted as the best of our own. Abuse, however, is abuse, whether it comes in the shape of vulgar bluster and threats, or whether it is couched in delicate phrases. The American press does not possess the happy art of expressing envy, malice, and all uncharitableness in terms of philanthropy and brotherly love; but the substance of its remarks sometimes reminds me of what I have read in the *Times.* It wields a bludgeon instead of a rapier; but it comes to the same whether your skull is broken or you are run through the body.

But, says the *Times,* there has been an entire absence of retaliation on the English side. Let me shortly recall some of the compliments to America which I have already quoted from the *Times.* The war, it said, was called by the North an anti-slavery war; this was for the most part a mere pretext to blind foreigners; so far as a desire for emancipation meant any-thing, it meant to cover designs of diabolical malignity; it was intended to lead to the organization of "a series of Cawnpores" (September 19, 1862), or to the total extirpa-tion of every white male in the South. The real motives of the war were far more commonplace; it was, in fact, a mere squabble for territory; in part due to a desire for protective tariffs unjustly favourable to the North, and having regard to the views of a large class, it might fairly be called a war "to keep slavery as one of the social elements of the Union." The desire for emancipation was "introduced into the war by an afterthought;" it served as a thin superficial varnish to vulgar, and sometimes to atrocious motives. In pursuing a wild will-of-the-wisp, the Northern armies, utterly unable to conquer the South, overmatched in states-manship, generalship, and courage, had made an easy conquest of their countrymen's liberties. The free, self-governing nation of English blood had become the humble slave of a despotism at once oppressive and ridiculous. Mob law had suppressed all that was noble and exalted in the nation, and was leading them to a fearful abyss of bankruptcy and ruin. The war had rapidly degenerated into a mere scramble for profits, kept up by profuse issues of paper money, and by a gigantic debt on which they did not even seriously intend to pay interest. Such as it was, the North would not fight in it themselves. They scraped together the refuse of Europe and stole the Southern negroes. Every boast which they had ever made was proved to be empty ; every taunt which they had aimed at Europe might be retorted upon themselves. An unrighteous war, in defiance of every principle upon which American government was based, would have no result but hopeless bankruptcy and the complete and final prostration of liberty. The republic had rotted into an empire, and the gangrene, as it elegantly expressed it, had burst.

This, forsooth, was not vituperation, because, I suppose, it was so obviously true. It is no abuse to call a chimney-sweep black ; but when he retorts, in his vulgar language, that you are a bloated aristocrat, and that he will whip you well when he has time for the job, he is indulging in " foolish vituperation." Or, perhaps, " vituperation " is too coarse a term to apply to the elegant language of the *Times* and its brethren. If I had proved that the *Times* had made a gigantic blunder from end to end as to the causes, progress, and consequences of the war, I should have done little. Its opinion might be proved worthless : but it would be merely worthless in the sense in which the old astronomers' notions of the solar system were worthless ; they did the solar system no harm. But I contend that I have proved simultaneously that it was guilty of " foolish vituperation," and as I am weak enough to think anything a serious evil which tends to alienate the freest nation of the old world from the great nation in the new, whose foundation is amongst our most glorious achievements, I contend, also, that I have proved the *Times* to be guilty of a public crime. It was, I admit, due to gross ignorance, and not to malice ; it may, I also admit, take such comfort as it can from the consideration that equal errors were committed in America ; but I still think its conduct criminal.

If, however, my previous statements should be insufficient, I will collect a few, and only a few, more specimens of what I under-

stand by abuse, pure and simple ; and I will show by one or two
examples what is the nature of the evil that may result. I will
quote nothing from that New York correspondent whose letters
are one long, tiresome tirade, that must, one would think, have
sickened even his employers. I will merely ask any one to tell
me whether the passages I am about to quote contain " foolish
vituperation," or what term can be found in the English language
that will more aptly describe them.

March 19, 1863—Contains a good specimen of the *Times*
" historical parallel style," in which " all history " is ransacked to
prove two platitudes and one false analogy. The platitudes are
that " States are not made in a day," and that " there is no crime
so ruinous as weakness or political rottenness." The parallel—
so obvious that one wonders it had never been previously suggested—is between North and South, on the one hand, and, on
the other, England and France when the sovereignty of France
was claimed by the kings of both countries. This ingenious
parallel is worked out at some length to help us to divine the
future of America. Meanwhile, we are told that " the hard
" metal and the sharp edge of a loftier nature and sterner will
" have cut into that great gangrene [the Union], as our old
" writers would have described it, and it has burst and gone."
The once United States are a mere heap of loose materials
" and caldron of molten stuff ready to receive whatever form
" fortune may determine." This is the general text. I will
now give some of the sermon.

Oct. 12, 1861. — " We regard this unnatural struggle with
" loathing and horror   .   .   .   the most groundless and wanton
" civil quarrel of which history gives us any account."

July 16, 1862.—" Even in America, credulous and simple as
" we may there seem to be when we say so, honesty would, we
" believe, be the best policy," and it dilates upon the systematic
falsification of contemporary history.

July 17.—The Americans are, it seems, "delighted with the great distress which has fallen upon our Lancashire operatives," they wish " to multiply the existing evil, to make it as wide and all-pervading as possible "—as was conclusively proved by the *George Griswold.*

July 18.—" The feeling is becoming very general that if we " .   .   .   . ought not to stop this effusion of blood by " mediation, we ought to give our moral weight to our English " kith and kin, who have gallantly striven so long for their liberties " against a mongrel race of plunderers and oppressors."

Aug. 12.—Mr. Roebuck's reviling " is so very like the truth " that it will probably be received with unbounded indignation. " Yet it is becoming, we are sure, the general opinion of Europe."

Feb. 20, 1863.—The notorious Manhattan is quoted and elaborately commented upon throughout an article as a fair specimen of " the fiercest Unionist and most uncompromising Northerner."   After quoting many of his ravings, the *Times* adds its hope that, " in speaking the language of the North, we " have improved our own tone, and manifested those generous " sympathies with an invader, which have been asked for at our " hands."

Jan. 20, 1863.—"A carnival of corruption"—"the people demoralized."

Jan. 26.—" No serious intention of repaying the loan at all."

May 21.—" The North have given no indications of sorrow or distress," in proof of which it appeals to the correspondent's letters.

I may remark upon this and similar accusations of heartlessness, that the *Times* never, so far as I have been able to discover, alludes to the most signal proof to the contrary, in that almost unequalled effort of private benevolence—the Sanitary Commission. People so heartless do not usually subscribe munificently to their sick and wounded.

May 28.—People "naturally asked whether the gentleman was
" to rule in the Old World and the opposite character in the New
" . . . it is vain to look for those higher principles from
" which alone we might expect a settlement of the question."
This pleasing article ends with the suggestion already quoted, that
the Americans should sometimes think what " ought" means.

June 18.—" Presumptuous folly, reckless fanaticism, gambling
cupidity to glut the avarice of a few obscure persons," are
attributed to the North.

Sept. 18.—"The Americans must be described as creatures of
" passion, without reason, or only that lower acuteness of under-
" standing which enables them to adapt means to their immediate
" ends." The Americans are ruled by blackguards (May 28); it
is natural to assume them to be brute beasts.

Indeed, as it attributed to them (July 11, 1862) the sentiment, " Evil, be thou my good," it may be said to have insinuated
their possession of some diabolic qualities.

Oct. 23.—America is in the hands of "brawlers, impostors, and
adventurers of every kind."

Jan. 22, 1864.—" The Southerners were daily told of a universal
" organization in which the will of the majority should override
" all Constitutions, all international law, all institutions, every
" right and interest that stood in its way. They dreaded—and it
" must be said, justly dreaded, the full brunt of that tyranny
" which they had long known, and which, it must be said, they
" had helped to create, but which they now saw about to be
" turned on themselves."

July 5, 1864.—(I may remark, as a characteristic circumstance,
that each previous Fourth of July had been marked by an article
exulting over the breakdown of all American anticipations, and
marked by such oratory as that of which I am giving specimens.)
" This war has been carried on with a cruelty far surpassing any-
" thing that can be laid to the charge of England. Towns have

" been burnt down in diabolical wantonness, the inhabitants of
" captured cities put to work in chains, universal plunder has
" impoverished the chief people of the conquered States, Congress
" has passed Confiscation Acts," &c. &c.   I have said nothing
as to charges of this nature, chiefly because I have the fear of
Colonel Crawley's case before my eyes, and know that to establish
the truth or falsehood of any charge about things happening at a
distance of several thousand miles would require an accumulation
of proofs for which I have not the means nor the time or space.
One remark must be made, which illustrates a special difficulty
under which I labour.   A false impression may be given more
easily and more safely by omission than commission.   Many
of the most grievous misrepresentations of the *Times* are due
to the art of omitting favourable circumstances.   It is hard,
however, for me to assert that hidden away in some of the
vast bulk of printed paper there may not lurk many statements
which I have failed to remark.   I know no means of giving
any adequate idea of the precise extent to which the darker
shades have been blackened, and the brighter omitted from the
picture.   I can only dwell upon positive faults in the outline.
I will, therefore, merely remark that whilst the *Times* frequently
alludes to alleged Federal atrocities, it passes with a tender
hand over those charged on similar evidence against the Confederates.   It speaks of General Macneile's execution of the
men in Missouri.   Indeed, the story so pleased the New York
correspondent that he related it at full length a second time
many months after its occurrence, with no intimation that it
was not a new occurrence.   But the *Times* scarcely mentions
Quantrell's atrocious massacre of the inhabitants of Lawrence.
I have found no reference to Forrest's massacre of negro troops
at Fort Pillow, though, whether false or true, the story was
supported by elaborate evidence.   Indeed, as I have said, the
only reference to a slaughter of negro prisoners is adduced as

a ground of attack upon Lincoln for raising negro troops. And I have found no allusion to that charge which, more than any other, tended to embitter the Northern feeling—that, namely, of the systematic ill-treatment of Northern prisoners. It may be exaggerated or false, though a full account of the evidence upon which it rests has been published, but it should have been noticed. It is a characteristic proceeding, by the way, of the New York correspondent, that he attributes the ferocity of the New York rioters in 1863 to the "cold-blooded brutality" of the Republican journals, which had remonstrated, very sensibly, it would seem, against the practice of firing blank cartridges to intimidate them.

These quotations will probably serve as sufficient examples of the tone adopted by the *Times* whenever the North was in a bad way; for if anything could add to the impression made by the abuse, it is the contrast afforded by occasional intervals of civility. I cannot fully go into this charge. I will just remark that the abuse increased in vigour from Fort Sumter up to the end of 1861, and the connection of the war with slavery was strongly denied. During the spring of 1862 the early successes of the North caused the *Times* to speak of it with decent civility. It " could hardly blame the North," it said (April 28), for seeking what it honestly believed to be its rights, though blindly. And it incidentally admitted the war to be due to slavery. (April 17.) —It was " caused by the deadly animosities of slaveholders and freemen," and " the effect of an attempt to unsettle the relations of master and slave." Again, the fortunes of the North declined till they reached their nadir in the spring of 1863. The *Times*, besides plentiful abuse, felt itself encouraged up to the pitch of admitting slavery to be connected with the Southern cause, and defending it as socially advantageous, and even as not opposed to the Bible. This I have already proved. As the North became victorious last spring they effected another strategetical movement.

Let me now take its treatment of one or two special points. I have shown incidentally what was the *Times'* opinion of President Lincoln.

Oct. 21, 1862.—It discussed the character of " Lincoln the Last," or " Honest Abe," " Honest to his party, not to his people." " Such honesty," it added, " is an intolerable evil." " How " insupportable must be the despotism in which a man of this " calibre is despot !" and it speculated on Lincoln's name being in future classed amongst those of " monsters, wholesale assassins and butchers."

I have also quoted enough to show the view they took of the great measure with which Lincoln's name will be for ever associated—the emanicipation proclamation. It was, at the time, supposed to be a cloak for a diabolical crime. It appeared afterwards to be a mere reckless bid for support. He was ready (January 12, 1863) to take " peace or war, or both at once ; " slavery or abolition, or both together ; he gives every principle a " chance," his one object being, it is to be supposed, to keep power.

Sept. 17, 1863.—It observed, " Strange that he should have " blundered and vacillated so long as he has without losing " confidence in himself, or altogether losing that of his " countrymen."

Sept. 24.—It explains that he is " really indifferent to slavery ; " it is his misfortune to have become under pressure of the " merciless philanthropist, an instrument for exterminating the " whites."

Dec. 23.—His inaugural message is " the most cold-blooded political document ever published."

I have found no traces of the *Times* abandoning this view of his character.

Nov. 22, 1864.—It remarked upon his re-election that we have no great reason to complain of Lincoln's course. " He has gone through the course of defying and insulting England, which is the traditional way of obtaining the Irish vote." But for his countrymen his re-election, as I have shown, means "the abandonment of the right of self-government," and all kinds of horrible things. In short, he was a blundering, unprincipled, cold-blooded despot.

On April 17, 1865, the *Times* remarked on his having chosen "the most odious and offensive topics that could be obtruded into a speech on reconstruction," and infers that the only hope for America is in the rise of a new race of statesmen.

The news came of his assassination, and two days afterwards (April 19) we are told Lincoln was "a man who could not under any " circumstances have been easily replaced." He "had won for " himself the respect and confidence of all." His "perfect " honesty had soon become apparent."

April 29.—Lincoln "was as little a tyrant as any man who " ever lived. He could have been a tyrant if he had liked, " but he never made so much as an ill-natured speech." He was " doubtless glad at last to see slavery perish, but his personal " opinions on that subject were not permitted to influence the " policy of the Government."

I will venture to say that I could not have contradicted the *Times* more flatly myself. The death of a great man naturally induces us to speak kindly of his memory. But it does not always induce us to contradict in terms every criticism we passed upon him till the day of his death. Either the praise must be hypocritical, or the abuse must have been ill founded. Probably both are worthless; and such compliments are more likely to provoke contempt than gratitude.

Let me notice the way in which the *Times* received the news of the first battle, in which an army of raw volunteers broke and fled in confusion after several hours' hard fighting, without food, under a hot sun, upon the unexpected arrival of hostile reinforcements.

The *Times* described (August 7, 1861) how " 75,000 American
" patriots fled for twenty miles in an agony of fear, although no
" one was pursuing them ; how 75,000 other patriots abstained
" from pursuing their 75,000 enemies because they were not
" informed how stark frightened they were." The artillery was not
captured, but picked up. This is all fair play. The comments
are the special beauty of the article. The Government, said
the *Times*, " will call out a few more millions of volunteers, and
" must make a confident demand upon the incredulous world for a
" few more hundred millions sterling." But at bottom there must
be a growing consciousness that " the Southern nut is too hard to
" crack ; that the military line as a matter of business does not
" answer." There will be " tall words," but " in the face of that
" screaming crowd, the grand army of the Potomac," they will be
useless. Some silly boasts had been made on a false report of a
Northern victory. The North, said the *Times*, expects to " chaw
us up," but " we are not fearful enough to be ferocious." When
at peace, they " will not be so bloodthirsty as they think ; or, if
they should be, they will not be so mischievous as they say."
Spain would be strong enough to deal with their navy, and
Canada has before now given a good account of Yankee invaders.
This kind of writing was admirably suited to soothe a wounded
national vanity, and increase the mutual esteem of the two
countries.

I will conclude with one example, to show the effect which the
Times was likely to produce upon international relations. The
period at which we approached most closely to a war was doubtless on the *Trent* affair. Mr. Bright charged the *Times*, in the
session of 1862, with having done its best to bring about a war.
It was hardly worth while to answer a gentleman who had just
made the ridiculous assertions to the Liverpool Chamber of
Commerce that cotton was to be first expected from Northern
successes, and that the war had given a deathblow to slavery.

The *Times*, however, condescended to say (February 18) " We
" expressed ourselves so mildly, so cautiously, so reservedly, with
" such thorough submission to the law of nations and the legal
" authorities, that for several days after the rebound of the tidings
" at America, its writers were proclaiming that England took it
" very quietly indeed." Let us see how matters really stood.

On November 28 the *Times* published an article in an irre-
proachable spirit. Its law perhaps was bad, but its intentions good. It stated that the seizure of the envoys was a
questionable proceeding; that it was irregular, the proper course
being to make prize of the *Trent*, and bring the question before
the courts; but, on the whole, it was not improbable that ·the
Americans were legally justified, and, if so, we should yield with
a good grace. It is not surprising that the Americans took at
first the same view more strongly, that they assumed that they
were certainly right; that their papers wrote a great deal of nonsense, retorting much of the abuse which our national organ had
heaped upon them, and that public meetings conducted by stump
orators welcomed Wilkes as a spirited assertor of the country's
honour.

On the 29th the *Times* found out that it had made a slip. The
law officers of the Crown decided that Mason and Slidell must
be demanded, and on December 2 the *Times* further announced
that a proper demand for their delivery had been sent. From
this time· till the middle of January, 1862, one leader, sometimes
two, and sometimes three, appeared daily in the *Times* discoursing
upon American affairs; and if any one wishes to practise the art
of irritating abuse, I recommend him to study these charming
productions.

The City article of the 30th had already remarked, with its
usual delicate appreciation of American institutions, its fear that
the decision of the matter would be taken out of the hands of the
Government by the mob. The leading article of the same day

implied that even this view was too favourable. There was, it admitted, "a possibility that the act was not expressly directed " by the Government." "We fear, however, that the Federal " Government had deliberately determined to seize the Southern " Commissioners," and, in support of this hypothesis, it gave an elaborate discussion of certain rumours as to the movements of Federal vessels. This was confirmed (Dec. 3) by the assertion that America refuses to show the slightest respect for inter-national law. "It is evident," it inferred, "that if England " should be found ready to eat dirt, there will be no lack of " Americans to cram it down her throat," and, indeed, without waiting to discover our capacity of swallow, they must have been ready to try, for it believed war to have been deter-mined upon long ago. The American newspapers had, of course, given food for abuse ; but, before hearing of the attitude taken by England, there had been a change in their tone of " a wholesome kind," and this is the way in which the *Times* moralizes upon it. (Dec. 9.)—We might, it says, be happy if we could trust to the "blank terror in some of those broadsheets that have " been breathing flames for some years past." " Because we had, " half grumbling and half in contempt, allowed them for some " years to tread rudely upon our corns and to elbow us dis-" courteously," they had thought that we should submit "to have " our noses tweaked in solemn form by Mr. Seward." Sheer cowardice had, it seems, improved them. Gradually, as the chances of peace increased, the *Times* grew more blustering and offensive. The war was gradually brutalizing both sides. The South were bad enough (Dec. 10), but still it appears (Dec. 17) that they were fighting "to emancipate themselves from the " tyranny of a degraded mob, elective judges, and elective " governors." " The natural course of financial sequences must " bring the civil war to an end." Without the addition of a foreign war, "the other difficulties must produce an immediate

collapse, and the peace which ensues upon utter exhaustion."
Encouraged by this, the *Times* gloats over the sight of the
Americans yielding to our invincible arms. (Dec. 26.)—" It would
" be amusing, if it were not painful, to see how the whole set
" of tricky politicians are preparing to meet the anger of the
" ' Britisher.' " It was indeed possible that, notwithstanding their
abject terror, a war might be brought about, to escape from the
war at home.

The more numerous party would expect to chaw England up.
A few anxious business men might be against it. The party who
object to the war, because it will embarrass the conquest of the
South, are balanced by the large party disgusted with the present
contest and anxious to get out of it by a war with England. We
all know, as the mob are the rulers of the United States,
whether " the few anxious business men " and the sincere fanatics
are likely to control the braggarts and dishonest politicians.
The *Times* argued anxiously and as long as possible that
war was highly probable. The tone of America had become
peaceful : as the *Times* put it (Jan. 2, 1862), "when the lion
" approaches the douar of the wandering Arab, the dogs of
" the encampment are silent from fear ;" but, as it con-
solingly added, " it is not certain that the men of that encamp-
" ment will give up the sheep for which he is roaring without a
" fight." It repudiated with indignation the weak proposals of
Lord Ebury and some weak-minded lovers of peace, who proposed
an arbitration. It bragged of our capacity to whip the Yankees
whenever we pleased. The Americans were ignorant of our power.
(January 3, 1862.)—"At privateering we, as being infinitely
" stronger, could do more.than they." Our privateers " would be
" as certain in the long run to beat theirs as our Royal Navy
" would be to beat their ships of war." A war, indeed, would,
" comparatively speaking, be sport to us, though death to them—
" their navy is scarcely more formidable than that of Italy or

" Spain." And throughout all this reckless abuse or bluster there is not one civil word nor one hint that any considerations of justice could possibly have any weight with Mr. Lincoln, Mr. Seward, or the American people. Mason and Slidell were surrendered, and the abuse of the *Times* was increased (if possible) in proportion to its sense of safety. The surrender, it assured us as soon as it was reported, was due not to Vattel and Bynkershoek, (Jan. 9, 1862)—" but to the promptitude with which we reinforced " Admiral Hughes' fleet and poured battalion after battalion into " Canada." The quarrel being over (Jan. 10) it observed, " we are " rather better friends than before." As, however, it is reported that the Northerner hates England twice as much as he loves the Union, we had better maintain our forces in Canada. Mason and Slidell were on their way to England, and the *Times* feared that they would receive what it calls an " ovation." It accordingly informed them (January 11, 1862), that " the general impression in this country is " that both sides in the States have acted as ill as could be . . . " that it is not for England to decide which of them bears the " palm for insolence, outrage, treachery, and folly." The quarrel was like one between two noisy brats in the nursery, which the mother is called in to quiet, and it draws this beautiful moral :—" Let us sincerely hope that our countrymen will not " give these fellows anything in the shape of an ovation. . . . " We should have done just as much to rescue two of their " own negroes. . . . So please, British public, let's have " none of these things." As a humble member of that collective unit, I shrink from the offensive familiarity of this *soi-disant* representative of my country as one shrinks from being patted on the back by a British snob in a foreign land. During the rest of January the *Times* absolutely coruscated with a succession of jubilant articles calculated to point out to the North their extreme folly and our serene wisdom.

In the presence of a national danger there are two lines of

policy possible. One is to abstain from studied insult, to give the American Government all the strength which a calm appeal to their sense of justice could confer, and whilst preparing for war, to seek by all honourable means for peace. But if policy is to be determined by the motive of pleasing your audience, and your audience is certain to be in a bad temper, then say all the insulting things you can think of. Tell the Americans that a deliberate breach of international law was all we expected of them; that we were ready to punish them like yelping curs; that we hoped nothing from their justice, but much from their cowardice; that even if their Government wished to be just, which is highly improbable, the mob would not permit it; fill all vacant spaces with well-worn topics of abuse; rake up all the old quarrels you can think of; and, if you don't promote peace, you will certainly sell your paper. I do not know how large a dose of this abuse reached America in time to influence the decision of the United States Government and people; but even if the *Times* can escape on the plea that it only used this language when it was tolerably safe, I would observe that it was not likely to make things pleasant for the next quarrel that might occur.

And this is my moral:—The persistent misapprehensions of the *Times* have, in my opinion, produced a very serious mischief. It was not that it took the Southern side. No American would have a right to complain if it had preferred the principle of State Rights to the abolition of slavery, although it is highly probable that many Americans would have complained and attributed it to mean jealousy. But-my complaint against the *Times* is that its total ignorance of the quarrel, and the presumption with which it pronounced upon its merits, led. to its pouring out a ceaseless flood of scurrilous abuse, couched, indeed, in decent language, but as essentially insulting as the brutal vulgarities of the *New York Herald*. No American—I will not

say with the feelings of a gentleman, for of course there are no
gentlemen in America—but no American with enough of the
common feelings of humanity to resent the insult when you spit
in his face could fail to be wounded; and, so far as he took the
voice of the *Times* for the voice of England, to be irritated
against England. I am not so vain as to think that anything
which I can do will at all lower the *Times* in popular esteem.
An attack upon its character for consistency and political
morality is pretty much thrown away ; it is like accusing a gipsy
of not having a clean shirt ; it has long learnt to be independent
of that luxury. If I had the eloquence of Burke my attacks
would be of little importance to the *Times.* Still, I am anxious
to do what little I can, not to injure the *Times,* but to explain
the true value of its criticism in this particular case. I
may help to prove to some Americans that the *Times* does not
express the judgment of thoughtful Englishmen, but only supplies
the stimulating, but intrinsically insipid fare that most easily titil-
lates an indolent appetite. Men whose opinions about America are
mere guesses lying on the surface of their minds, and never subject
to its serious operations, like this kind of stuff. That is true, but
that is all that is to be said ; and I see no reason why a sensible
American should be vexed by such random ignorance. All that I
can profess to do for English readers is, to give an additional
proof of the correctness of the common opinion about the *Times,*
namely, that, as for consistency, it has none, and its politics are
altogether uncertain.

It is probable that the interests of foreign politics may continue to increase. Personal observation in America has shown
me the pernicious effect which the *Times* may produce upon our
relations with other countries. The cruel insults to men, who,
at least, were patriotic to the pitch of enthusiasm, were supposed
to come from the English nation ; and every concession became
doubly difficult. If future complications should arise, any

contribution towards a due appreciation of the *Times* may be valuable.

I will only add that I have been quite unable to give a complete picture of the *Times*, and, especially, to give any adequate idea of its abuse. I have gathered a few pearls on the shore of the great ocean of misrepresentation. I cannot hope that any one will feel their full force who does not remember that they are mere specimens, and that the effect of steady abuse accumulates like the effect of the drops of water falling on to the head of a prisoner in the Inquisition.

THE END.

Printed by Jas. Wade, 18, Tavistock-street, Covent-garden.

JOHN BYROM.

Who was John Byrom? That is a question to which, if it were set in an examination for students of English literature, an answer might reasonably be expected; but which, if put to less omniscient persons, might not improbably receive a rather vague reply. And yet an answer might be given which would awake some familiar associations. John Byrom was the author of two or three epigrams which for some reason have retained their vitality well into a second century of existence. The unmusical are still happy to recall the comparison between Handel and Buononcini, and to wonder that there should be such a difference between "tweedle-dum and tweedle-dee," though they are apt to assign to Swift instead of Byrom the credit of being the first worm to turn against the contempt of more happily endowed natures. There is the still more familiar verse; ending :

> "But who Pretender is, and who is King,
> God bless us all, that's quite another thing."

And there is a certain assault upon "Bone and Skin, two millers thin," which—though the real names of the millers and the circumstances which induced the declaration that flesh and blood could not bear them have long vanished out of all but antiquarian memories—have somehow continued to go on jingling in men's ears ever since 17th December, 1728. I have said enough to suggest more than one problem. What is the salt which has kept these fragments of rhyme so long alive ? Is it due to the sound or the sense ? Survival for a century has been given as the test which entitles a man to be called a classic. Does the survival of these little impromptus entitle Byrom to be a classic ? May we call them pearls five lines long, that are to sparkle on the stretched forefinger of all time ? That seems to be too lofty a claim. The thought is not by itself very subtle or very keen. And yet when we think how few are the writers who can blow even the frailest of wordbubbles which shall go floating down five or six generations, we must admit the fact to be remarkable. What is the quality which it indicates in the author ? And here I might affect to take up the psychological method, show what are the peculiarities

necessarily implied by success in these little achievements; deduce
from them what must have been the characteristics of Byrom's
mind and temperament; and finally, by appealing to facts, show
how strikingly the *à priori* reasoning would be confirmed by
experience. I think that a little ingenuity might enable an
ambitious critic to give plausibility to such a procedure; but I
prefer to take a humbler method, for which sufficient materials have
been lately provided. Byrom, I may remark, in the first place, is
hardly thought, even by his warm admirers, to be other than a
second-rate poet: now, need I appeal to the Latin grammar to prove
that second-rate poetry is not generally worth reading? The reason
is, I suppose, that a second-rate poet only does badly what has been
done well, whereas even a tenth-rate historian or philosopher may
be giving something new. That reason, at least, will do sufficiently
well to suggest why an exception may be made in favour of some
second-rate poetry. There are cases in which poetry not of the
highest class reveals a peculiar charm of character. We cannot
help loving the writer, though we admit that he was not a Dante, or a
Shakespeare, nor even—in this case the comparison is more to the
purpose—a Pope. The first condition of this kind of charm is, of
course, perfect simplicity. The poet must be really showing us his
heart, not getting upon stilts and trying to pour out epic poems and
Pindaric odes, after the fashion of some of Byrom's contemporaries.
Glover's *Leonidas* and Mason's odes have long been swept into the
limbo where such things go; but the excellent Byrom, who is content to be himself, and whose self happened to be a very attractive
one, may be still read with pleasure. Indeed, and this is what
prompts me to speak of him just now, he has found an editor who
reads him with enthusiasm as well as pleasure. Four handsome
volumes* have recently been published by the Chetham Society under
the care of Dr. Ward, principal of the Owen's College. Dr. Ward
has done his work in the most loving spirit; he has pointed out with
affectionate solicitude everything that strikes him as admirable in
Byrom's poetry; he has not been so blinded by zeal as to try and
force upon us admiration for the weaker pieces at the point of the
critical bayonet; and he has given with over-flowing learning everything that a reader can possibly require for the due appreciation of
incidental circumstances. I fear that I am not quite a worthy
follower; my admiration of Byrom's poetry stops a little further this
side of idolatry; and, therefore, I frankly admit that Dr. Ward is
likely to be a better guide than I to those who are accessible to
Byrom's charm. In such cases excess of zeal is far less blamable
than defect. Still, I hope that in a liking for Byrom himself
I am not altogether unworthy to follow in his admirer's steps;

* Two volumes, each in two parts, properly.

and it is of the man himself that I propose chiefly to speak. Byrom, as I think, is a very attractive example of a charming type of humanity; and shows qualities really characteristic of the period, though too often overlooked in our popular summaries. He flourished during the literary reigns of Addison and Pope; and the splendour of their fame is too often allowed to blind us to the peculiarities of some of the secondary luminaries.

Byrom has already been made known to us by his "remains," published for the Chetham Society some forty years ago. Of this, Dr. Ward says that, were it more widely known, it would be "one of the most popular works of English biographical literature." It is, I think, only fair to warn anyone who is tempted to rush at once to a library to procure this fascinating work, that it will not yield up its charm—a charm there certainly is—without a certain amount of perseverance. A good deal of it is a skeleton diary—mere statements of small facts, which, if interesting at all, are interesting only when you have enabled yourself to clothe the dry bones with the flesh and blood of reflection—and, moreover, Byrom is apt to be tantalizing, and to confine himself to brief notes just where we should be glad of a little more expansion. He meets·Laurence Sterne, for example, and repeats not a word of his talk. After making this reservation, I can fully agree with Dr. Ward, that it is impossible to read through the book without deriving a charming impression of Byrom himself, and of the circle in which he especially delighted.

And now I will try to answer briefly the question from which I started. Who was Byrom? Byrom was the descendant of an old family long settled near Manchester. The Byroms of Byrom had dwindled down till they were represented by one Beau Byrom, who, in the time of his cousin, was consuming the last payments of the ancestral estates, was subsiding into a debtor's prison, and was not above accepting a half-crown from his more prosperous relative. The Byroms of Manchester were meanwhile prospering in business. Manchester was then a country town of some 30,000 inhabitants, beginning to take a certain interest in a Bill permitting a freer use of cotton; but not, as yet, feeling itself aggrieved by exclusion from a Parliamentary representation. The upper classes had a strong tincture of the Jacobitism prevalent in the Lancashire of those days; and John, born in 1692, was clearly brought up in this faith. He was sent to Trinity College, Cambridge, then under the rule of the great Bentley, who was at the time beginning the famous legal warfare which was to display his boundless pugnacity and fertility of resource in litigation. Nobody was less inclined to sympathize with excessive quarrelsomeness than Byrom; but the young man, who became scholar and fellow of his college, was always on most friendly terms with the master. Bentley could be good company when his antipathies were not aroused ; and Byrom was welcomed to the great man's domestic circle. Incidentally this led to the performance which made him in a modest way famous for years to come. *The Spectator* had been revived in 1714, when Byrom was about to gain his fellowship. The young man sent a couple of 'papers which were published in the famous journal—a success sufficient to give him a kind of patent of authorship. He followed it up by the more successful "pastoral," addressed to Phebe. Phebe was Joanna or "Jug" Bentley, the master's youngest daughter. She was destined to be the mother of the Cumberland, described by Goldsmith as "*The Terence of England, the mender of hearts;*" but perhaps better known as Sheridan's *Sir Fretful Plagiary.* She was, as her son intimates, a witty young lady, sometimes coy and silent, and sometimes a little too smart in her satire. More than one of the college fellows were fascinated by her in later days, and even brought to take her father's side in his disputes. One of the superseded laments* her

> " haughtiness of mien,
> And all the father in the daughter seen."

At this period, though she was only eleven, she probably showed symptoms enough of these characteristics to suggest the tone of Byrom's famous verses. Famous they certainly were in his day, for his friends constantly ask him for copies; but perhaps they are not so famous now as to forbid a specimen. Colin is terribly put out by Phebe's absence.

> " My dog I was ever well pleaséd to see
> Come wagging his tail to my fair one and me :
> And Phebe was pleased too, and to my dog said,
> ' Come hither, poor fellow,' and patted his head.
> But now, when he's fawning, I with a sour look
> Cry ' Sirrah,' and give him a blow with my crook ;
> And I'll give him another ; for why should not Tray
> Be as dull as his master when Phebe's away?"

"I'll give him another," is a phrase for which I have often been grateful to the excellent Byrom. It gives a pleasant sanction to one's own humours. Though the metre limps a little in this stanza, it is often very dexterously used by Byrom; and the poem is worthy of a high place in the age of Mat Prior. Probably, though an absurd construction has been put upon the facts, the master was not the less friendly towards the young fellow for this compliment to his bright little daughter. "Mr. Spectator" judged rightly that it would divert his readers; and a Mr. Mills, years afterwards, "kissed the book" when he read it.

Byrom had some difficulty at the time in taking the oaths to the

* See his poem in *Nichol's Literary Anecdotes,* i., 244.

new family; and he made a rather mysterious journey soon afterwards to Montpelier. He professed to be studying medicine, and was afterwards often called "doctor." It was, however, strongly suspected that his journey had a political purpose. He certainly kissed the Pretender's hand at Avignon. He returned after a time to Manchester, where, in 1721, he married his cousin Elizabeth Byrom. His father was dead; and the family property had gone to his elder brother. Byrom was therefore in want of money, and the measure which he took for obtaining supplies was characteristic and led him into a peculiar career. Byrom would not have been the man he was without a hobby. In fact, he so far shared the spirit of the Shandy family that he had a whole stable of hobbies. He belongs on one side to the species which has been celebrated by so many of the eighteenth century humorists. He would have appreciated Sir Roger de Coverley, or Parson Adams, or Uncle Toby, or the Vicar of Wakefield. The kindly simplicity which takes a different colouring in each of those friends of our imagination was fully realized in Byrom. He was evidently overflowing with the milk of human kindness; attaching himself to every variety of person, from the great Bentley to the burlesque Sam Johnson, author of *Hurlothrumbo;* appreciating them as cordially as Boswell, and alienated by nothing but censorious harshness. But, through all, he has a quaint turn of mind which shows alternately the two aspects of genuine humour; a perception of the absurd side of other people's crotchets, or an addiction to some pet crotchet of his own. Now the great discovery upon which he prided himself was a system of shorthand. He had, it seems, invented a system in combination with a friend at college; and he now bethought himself of turning this invention to account. Shorthand was by no means a novelty; and we all remember how Pepys had turned it to account; but Byrom's was, so he believed, the very perfection of shorthand—"Beauty, Brevity, and Perspicuity" were, he says, its characteristics. He set about propagating the true faith with infinite zeal. In London he found a rival, one Weston, who was making a living by giving lessons in the art. Weston challenged him to display his skill, and put bragging advertisements in the papers to claim superiority. Byrom felt that his dignity might be compromised by a contest with a commonplace teacher. His own shorthand was founded on scientific principles and was a mystery to be imparted to the nobility and gentry, whereas Weston was a mere empiric, and moreover, a vulgar person who talked broad Scotch. Byrom, therefore, retorted only by some humorous remarks, and apparently made peace with his humble rival. He served as umpire at a contest between Weston and another pretender to the art, and laid down the law with the lofty superiority of a fellow of the Royal Society. When invited to take notes at a famous law case in those days he doubts his own ability and even recommends a trial of Weston. His own shorthand was too good, he seems to imply, to be exposed to the vulgar test of mere speed of writing. Experts, in fact, say that its defects in this respect led to its being superseded in the next generation. Meanwhile, however, Byrom not only believed himself, but collected a body of believers. They formed a shorthand society; they had periodical meetings, and addressed each other as "brothers in shorthand." Byrom was greeted as Grand-Master, and pronounced a solemn oration at their first gathering. Its preparation during two or three previous weeks is noted in his journals. He takes the highest possible tone. He humorously traces back his art to the remotest antiquity; he intimates that Plato probably used shorthand to take down the conversation of Socrates, and finds shorthand even in Egyptian hieroglyphics. The divine Tully, however, is his great model, and he shows by an ingenious emendation (notare for natare) that the Emperor Augustus taught his nephews not to swim, but to take notes. He points out that amidst all the vices of Caligula, one which was thought to deserve notice was his ignorance of shorthand. Making a rapid bound over the intervening period, with one brief touch at the Abbot Trithemius, he appeals to the patriotism of his hearers to support what was at this time held to be a specially English art. A formal paper is drawn up, beginning, *Quod felix faustum que sit* and declaring that the signers will form a society, *ad tachygraphiam nostram ediscendam promovendam et perpetuandam in secula seculaorum, 'Amen.*

The meetings of the shorthanders naturally took place at taverns, and they formed a kind of club after the fashion of the day. Byrom took five guineas from each aspirant to the art, and a promise not to divulge the secret. They had apparently very pleasant meetings, and diverged from shorthand into discussions of politics, theology, free-will, and things in general. On one occasion, for example, when Byrom observes that he was in "a talking humour," which was certainly not rare, he discusses the Babylonian and Coptic letters, the probabilities of the devil being saved, and "Dr. Dens' drawer of daggers." Unluckily, the remarks which threw light upon these topics are not reported. The society seems to have done its duty in loyally spreading its president's fame. Great men became his pupils. The most famous in early years was Lord Chesterfield; Horace Walpole afterwards took some lessons. His warmest friend was the amiable philosopher, David Hartley, who cordially supported him in efforts to raise a subscription for a publication of his method once for all. Although this came to nothing, Byrom, in 1742, obtained an Act of Parliament which gave him the right of publishing and teaching for twenty-one years.

It was while he was engaged upon this propaganda that most of the diary was written. Manchester, of course, did not afford aspirants enough to maintain a teacher. Byrom had, therefore, to leave his family and pass months together in London and at Cambridge, where he had kept up many friendships. Travelling, of course, was a serious business. He generally makes two days of the fifty miles from London to Cambridge, though he once does it without an upset in less than nine hours. Now and then there is mention of a coach, but he is generally on horseback. Sometimes he rides post on "little hobbling horses," which leave him with aching arms after forty or fifty miles. Oftener it seems that he buys a horse at Manchester for five pounds or so, and sells it when he gets from London, and his horses are apt to turn out blind or lame. Once he collects a party of half-a-dozen friends and makes a walking tour from London, through Oxford, Worcester, and Shrewsbury to Manchester. It is to be regretted that he scarcely gives more than glimpses of these little tours. They suggest dimly the days when the wanderer had to plunge through labyrinths of muddy lanes; when he had to take a guide from one halting-place to another, and make enquiries of knowing persons as to the proper turning where you should leave the great northern road to diverge to Manchester. I see no indications, either here or in the poems, that the excellent Byrom cared for "nature" in the shape of scenery. He had none of the love for field sports—which in those days might serve as an excuse for enjoying the country. "Nay," he observes, when someone sends him a hare,

> " Nay, should one reflect upon cruelty's source,
>   In the gentlemen butchers, the Hunt, and the Course,
>   'Twere enough to prevent either pudding or jelly
>   From storing such carcase within a man's belly ! "

Here and there he has an adventure. He has a gift for falling in with the most deserving beggars, poor soldiers who have been "in slavery" somewhere, and the like; and gives them money and letters to his friends. Once, in Epping Forest, on the way to Cambridge, he has the proper meeting with a highwayman. Of course, he takes it good-humouredly, as an excellent pretext for a copy of verses. The highwayman's bad language runs spontaneously into rhyme; and in proper epical style the ruffian is put to flight by the mock-heroic vision of the " Goddess Shorthand, bright celestial maid ! " In sober prose, the highwayman goes off with a guinea of Byrom's, and Byrom expects to see him again in the neighbour-

hood of Tyburn. Byrom, however, is really happy when he is in
the full stream of society. One of his friends describes a typical
London day from imagination, which, as the diary shows, is very
nearly correct. He generally gets up late, we are sorry to observe,
but he has often been sitting up at a club, or sometimes studying
Hebrew till two or three in the morning. He has a meagre dish of
tea, reads the equally meagre papers, and groans over his absence
from Mrs. Byrom and his family. Then he turns out to give a lesson
in shorthand. He is tempted to "a hedge-booksellers in some
bye-lane." He is in the habit of denouncing the love of book-buy-
ing as a vanity, but he cannot resist it. He buys some queer old
volume—mystical divinity if possible—and, to do him justice, sel-
dom gets to a pound and often descends to fourpence. Afterwards
he drops in upon friendly Dr. Hartley and his charming wife, and
discusses the chances of a subscription for his book. He fills up
time by an interview with a member of some eccentric sect ; and,
finally, meets a knot of friends at a tavern. Byrom, of course, was
strictly temperate, though he seems to have tried his digestion by
some rather odd mixtures (such as cream and ale), and equally, of
course, he is, though not quite systematically, a vegetarian. He would
have been an anti-vaccinationist, and already denounces inocula-
tion. His friends dearly like to pay him little compliments by
asking for a copy of "My time, O ye Muses," or his epigram on
Handel and Buononcini. Now and then he extemporizes a copy of
verses on the appearance of the president of a club, for example, in
" a black bob-wig." What can be the cause ?

> " A phrenzy ? or a periwigmanee
> That overruns his pericranie ? "

That he could enjoy some amusements which seem scarcely in
character is proved by the verses on Figg and Sutton—done into
prose in Thackeray's *Virginians,* and Dr. Ward has to remind us
that this was " not a brutal prize-fight," but an ultra vigorous
" assault-at-arms." The line seems rather hard to draw. Byrom at
least sympathizes with the familiar sentiment about the " British
Grenadier."

> " Were Hector himself, with Apollo to back him,
> To encounter with Sutton,—zooks ! How he would thwack him !
> Or Achilles, though old Mother Thetis had dipt him,
> With Figg—odds my life ! how he would have unript him ! "

Another of Byrom's characteristic performances was prompted by
his interest in his fellow townsman, Samuel Johnson, a fiddler and
dancing master, who produced a strange medley called *Hurlothrumbo.* Dr. Ward, who has read it, as in duty bound, says that
it is sheer burlesque, though some critics seem to be haunted by an

uncomfortable suspicion that its apparent madness conceals some sparks of genius. Anyhow, Byrom took it as farce, and partly for the fun of the thing, and partly from a good-natured wish to be of use to the author, contributed an amusing epilogue and attended the first performance in London. There were seven or eight "garters" in the pit; Byrom led the *claque*. The audience took the joke. The play ran for thirty nights; the name got a place in popular slang, and Johnson appears to have been grateful, whether he quite perceived or not that Byrom was laughing in his sleeve. "For my part," says Byrom to his wife, "who think all stage entertainments stuff and nonsense, I consider this as a joke upon 'em all."

This, indeed, marks Byrom's peculiar vein. Hitherto, I have spoken of him as an admirably good-natured humorist and lover of harmless fun. He can go to a tavern or Figg's "amphitheatre" and, to all appearance, throw himself into the spirit of the performances as heartily as any of his companions. Yet, at the same time, he was a man of very deep and peculiar religious sentiments. In this matter of the play, he gradually came, it seems, to take a stricter view. The denunciation of the stage by the nonjuror, Jeremy Collier, had become famous. Arthur Bedford, an orthodox clergyman, had (in 1719) collected 7,000 "immoral sentiments from British dramatists" to prove the same point, and William Law, Byrom's great teacher, had demonstrated in a treatise the absolute unlawfulness of stage entertainments (1726), and had elsewhere declared that "the play-house was as certainly the house of the devil as the church was the house of God." Byrom was, perhaps, one of those people who could not be too hard even upon the "puir de'il." He was, at least, willing to try the effect of good-humoured raillery on the evil one before proceeding to stronger measures. When one of his friends complained of Law's severity, Byrom is evidently puzzled. His reverence for Law struggles with a sense that in this case the oracle was rather harsh. But in other matters Byrom's loyalty was boundless. Byrom's interest in various representatives of the religious speculations of the time is shown constantly in his diaries. He meets William Whiston, the successor to Newton's professorship, who had been deprived of his place as a heretic, and went about in all societies (he appears in the well-known picture of Tunbridge Wells with Richardson, Chesterfield, and the rest) trying to propagate what he took to be primitive Christianity. Dr. Primrose, as we know, was unlucky enough to be converted to his doctrine of monogamy. In simplicity and honesty he was worthy to make friends with Byrom; but, to say the truth, he appears in the diary rather in the character of a conceited bore. He had not Byrom's saving sense of humour. Then there was

Edward Elwall, who was tried for blasphemy because he taught the
"perpetual obligation" of the Jewish law, and consequently wore a
beard and a Turkish habit (the last out of respect, we are told, for
the Mahommedans), and shut his shop on Saturdays. King George,
he said, according to Dr. Johnson, if he were afraid to dispute with
a poor old man, might bring a thousand of his blackguards with
him; and, if that would not do, a thousand of his red guards. He
seems, however, to have got out of his troubles, and was duly in-
terviewed by Byrom. Byrom met more remarkable personages.
He knew something of the Wesleys, and he had one of the few re-
corded interviews with Bishop Butler. They had a long discussion
as to the claims of reason and authority. The bishop, one may
guess, got rather the best of it, as Byrom admits that he was himself too warm, while the bishop was conspicuously mild and candid.
Unluckily, Byrom was an inadequate Boswell, and is so anxious to
record his own argument on behalf of authority that he does
not quite let us know what Butler had to say for reason. Law,
however, is by far the most conspicuous figure. Law, when
Byrom first went to see him (4th March, 1729), was living
in the house of old Mr. Gibbon at Putney, and acting as tutor
to the younger Gibbon, afterwards father of the historian. He had
been at Cambridge in Byrom's time, had got into difficulties for his
Jacobite proclivities, and, by refusing to take the oaths, had cut
himself off from an active clerical career. Byrom would sympathize with him upon this ground; but it was the recently published
Serious Call which led to the new connexion. Byrom bought the
book in February, 1729, and at once felt the influence, which made
its perusal a turning-point in the lives of many eminent men of the
day. To him it was especially congenial. Law afterwards became
a disciple of Jacob Böhme, and Byrom, though he accepted the
later utterances with reverence, confessed that they were above his
comprehension. Of such matters, I may say that at a later period
Law might probably have been, like Coleridge, a follower of
Schelling, and have clothed his thought in the language of trans-
cendental metaphysics rather than of the old theosophy. He was
no mere dreamer or word-maker. If to his contemporaries he
seemed to be talking mere jargon, later critics have thought that
his position showed a real insight into the intellectual deficiencies
of the time. But, in any case, he was, as Gibbon declares, "a wit
and a scholar"; had not his mind been "clouded with enthusiasm" he would have been one of the most agreeable authors of
the day; and his portraits in the *Serious Call* are "not unworthy
of the pen of La Bruyère." These compliments from Gibbon are
significant. Neither Law nor Byrom were contemporaries of
Addison and Pope for nothing. However far they were from the

ordinary tone of religion and philosophy, they could both mix in
the society of the day; and write as brightly and observe as keenly
as the ordinary frequenter of clubs and coffee-houses. Their
mysticism was not mere muddle. They show that a man may
have the sparkle and clearness of the wits of Queen Anne allied
with a steady flow of sweet and tender sentiment.

Byrom had already shown his fitness to be a disciple of Law.
One of his pleasantest copies of verses tells how, in 1727, he
bought a picture of Malebranche, a philosopher naturally revered
by both. Byrom describes his eagerness in going to the auction,
his palpitations when the portrait of the great teacher was brought
out, the haste with which he advanced his biddings, and how he gets
the picture for three pounds five shillings. His ecstasy is inde-
scribable! Let your duchesses throw away ten times as many
guineas on pictures of nobodies by famous artists. Byrom has got
his Malebranche, "the greatest divine that e'er lived upon earth,"
whips into a coach, calls to the driver to go as fast as he can spin;
deposits the treasure at his chambers, and summons his friend to
come and rejoice; let him bring a friend or two to "mix metaphysics, and shorthand, and port." What, he exclaims, can "be
more clever?"

"Huzza! Father Malebranche, and Shorthand for ever!"

The *Serious Call* inspired another poem. When Byrom, a few
days after reading it, made his first call upon the author, he had
in his pocket a versification of a quaint parable which it contains. Law compares the man whose heart is set upon the world
to a person with a monomania about a pond. He passes his life in
trying to keep the pond full, and is finally drowned in it. This
struck Byron's fancy. He expands it into a fable in verse, and
ventures to show his performance to Law himself. Law laughed
and begged him not to turn the whole book into verse, "for
then it would not sell in prose—so the good man can joke." This
was before the rise of the Authors' Society. In later days Law
encouraged Byrom to versify other works, and seems to have
thought that the effect would be to advertize the prose. He calls
Byrom his laureate.

Byrom, I suspect, did not contribute much to Law's popularity.
The poems had not a large circulation. Some of his other religious
poems have great merits. Of an early paraphrase of the 23rd Psalm
I will only say that Dr. Ward endorses the statement of a Mr.
Hedges, that he "would give all the world to have been able to
have done them." It is in the same metre as the pastoral, and like
that poem owes its charm to the entire simplicity which enables
Byrom as a reverential interpreter to catch the charm of that
masterpiece of Hebrew poetry. Another poem,

" Christians awake ! salute the happy morn,
   Whereon the Saviour of the world was born,"

has been often reprinted, and is given in Hymns Ancient and
Modern. I may infer that it is quite as familiar to my readers as
to myself. It probably marks Byrom's highest level, though some
other of his religious poems, especially those in which he cele-
brates his favourite virtue, contentment, have the same charm.
They breathe, at least, the sweetness and simplicity of the writer's
own character. I will quote one little fragment as at once brief
and characteristic :—

" O happy Resignation !
   That rises by its fall !
   That seeks no 'exaltation.
   But wins by losing all ;
   That conquers by complying,
   Triumphing in its lot ;
   That lives when it's a-dying,
   And is when it is not ! "

The longer pieces, in which Byrom versified Law's works with
more or less closeness, come nearer to the conventional style of the
period, and drop pretty frequently into the flat of mere rhymed
prose. One of the longer, upon " Enthusiasm," may be mentioned
as symptomatic of Byrom's position. Our ancestors understood by
" enthusiasm " the state of mind of the fanatical sects of the Commonwealth, or of the "French Prophets" of the eighteenth century.
An enthusiast meant a believer in a sham inspiration. The
gradual change of the word to a complimentary meaning marks
the familiar change, which was also shown by the development
of sentimentalism in literature. Byrom, following Law pretty
closely, takes " enthusiasm " to mean devotion to some end, and is
good or bad, according to the goodness or badness of the end.
Everybody must have some aim. The enthusiasm which he shared
with Law meant a serious belief in Christianity, and the worldly
only scoffed because they were equally enthusiastic about some
really inferior aim. A few verses will show how far Byrom could
follow in the steps of Pope. Expanding a sentence of Law's, he
compares the classical enthusiast with the Christian. The scholar
is grieved when he sees,

" Time, an old Goth, advancing to consume
   Immortal Gods and once eternal Rome ;
   When the plain Gospel spread its artless ray
   And rude uncultured Fishermen had sway ;
   Who spared no Idol, tho' divinely carved,
   Tho' Art and Muse and Shrine-engraver starved ;
   Who saved *poor wretches* and destroyed, *alas!*
   The vital marble and the breathing brass.
   Where does all Sense to him and Reason shine ?
   Behold, in Tully's rhetoric divine !

'Tully'! Enough ; high o'er the Alps he's gone,
To tread the ground that Tully trod upon ;
Haply, to find his statue or his bust,
Or medal green'd with Ciceronian rust ;
Perchance, the Rostrum—yea, the very wood
Whereon this elevated genius stood.
When forth on Catiline, as erst he spoke,
The thunder of ' *Quousque tandem* ' broke. "

Byrom is beginning to forget even Tully's merits as a shorthand writer. He follows Law towards the condemnation, not only of the stage, but of classical scholarship and art in general.

It does not appear, however, that Byrom ever got quite so far. Law retired to his curious hermitage at King's Cliffe, where he could abandon himself to pious meditation and the demoralization of the neighbourhood by profuse charity. Byrom was held fast by his domestic ties; and took an interest in the local politics of Manchester. His talent for versification gave him frequent employment. He contributed a number of verses, in the nature of election squibs, to a newspaper of the period, and whenever he had an argument with a friend, he twists his logic into verse. Some of the results are quaint enough. Tempted, apparently, by Bentley's example, he had made a variety of conjectural emendations of Horace, obviously rash if not altogether absurd. But it could have entered into no less whimsical head to put the arguments for them into rhyme. He suggests *unum* for *nonum* in the familiar passage,

" I take the correction, *unumque prematur*
' Let it lie for one twelvemonth '—Ah, that may hold water ! "

and argues the point through twelve eight-lined stanzas. Another " poem " is an antiquarian discussion, showing that St. Gregory and not St. George was the patron saint of England ; he proves in another that the locusts eaten by the Baptist were fruit, not insects; in a third, that the miracle at the Pentecost was worked upon the hearers, not the speakers.

" ' Are not these,' said the men, the devout of each land,
' Galileans that speak, whom we all understand ?'
As much as to say, ' By what wonderful powers
Does the tongue Galilean become to us ours ?' "

With equal readiness he enters into an elaborate exegetical discussion, defending Sherlock against Conyers Middleton ; expounds the orthodox doctrine of the fall of man and justification by faith ; condemns Jonathan Edwards' arguments upon free-will, or versifies some prayer or letter that has struck him in reading memoirs or treatises of mystical divinity. The worthy Byrom, it must be added, did not take his own performances in this line too seriously. They were an amusement—a quaint whim characteristic of an oddly constituted brain; and one fancies that when he forces even Hebrew and Greek into the fetters of his "cantering rhymes," and twists dry grammatical discussion into comic metres, he feels that the process takes the bitterness out of controversy and enables him to treat thorny subjects in a vein of pleasantry. It is characteristic that he came into collision with the colossal Warburton, who had treated Law with his usual brutality, and that even Warburton found it desirable for once to be civil to so amiable an antagonist.

Byrom's activity in the shorthand business declined after the death of his brother in 1740 gave him the family estates. In 1745 he was presented to the Chevalier in Manchester; but luckily did not commit himself in any dangerous way to answering his own question, Which was King and which was Pretender? Byrom was very near the Quakers in such matters. In a poem on the occasion his hero, representing Lancashire in dialect and common-sense, decides, in spite of patriotic taunts, to look after his own carcase and leave Highlanders and redcoats to fight it out. Byrom obviously approves. Nobody, as other poems prove, could be less given to the worship of Jingo. He tried vainly to save some young friends, less prudent than himself, convicted of joining the rebels—and, of course, wrote his petition in verse. He protested, too, in verse, and with equal want of success, against the denunciators of Admiral Byng. He died a few years later (1763). He was not buried as the law directed, in woollen. His executors had to pay £5 as a fine. As Byrom does not appear to have left any verses to justify the failure we may perhaps assume that the omission was not due to any final whim of his own. He would hardly have missed such a chance for a poem. Few kindlier men have been buried either in woollen or linen.

LESLIE STEPHEN.

HENRY SIDGWICK.

[*Off-printed from* MIND: *a Quarterly Review of Psychology and Philosophy. Vol. X., N.S., No. 37.*]

BY LESLIE STEPHEN.

HENRY SIDGWICK.

[*Off-printed from* Mind : *a Quarterly Review of Psychology and Philosophy.* Vol. X., N.S., No. 37.]

By Leslie Stephen.

I have undertaken after some hesitation the task of writing an obituary notice of Henry Sidgwick for this journal, which owes so much to him both as a contributor and, for many years, as a financial supporter. I could not now try, even if I held myself to be more competent than I am, to give any estimate of his work in philosophy. Readers of Mind have formed their own judgment in that matter. I am, however, qualified to say something of the man, partly because I was for many years honoured by his friendship; and more because I have been enabled to fill up the gaps in my own knowledge by the help of those who were in closer relations to him.[1] Though I hope that I did not wholly fail to appreciate Sidgwick during his lifetime, I can now see, not without regret, that I had scarcely recognised to the full the singular merits of one of the purest and loftiest natures of our generation. I think, too, that a clear appreciation of

[1] Mrs. Sidgwick has been so good as to give me information and has, in particular, allowed me to make use of a brief autobiographical fragment, written during his last illness, from which I have quoted some sentences. I have also to express my warm thanks to Mr. Arthur Sidgwick, to Dr. Jackson of Trinity College, to Dr. Venn of Caius, to Prof. Ward and to Prof. Maitland. Interesting notices by the Master of Christ's College (in the *Cambridge Review* for 25th October); by Sir F. Pollock (in the *Pilot* for 15th September); by Mr. Masternan (in the *Commonwealth* for October) have also been useful.

the man will throw some light upon the philosopher, though
I must be content to indicate very briefly the general result.

Henry Sidgwick, born 31st May, 1838, was the third (and
second surviving) son of the Rev. William Sidgwick.   The
father was the son of a cotton-spinner at Skipton, graduated
at Cambridge in 1829, married Miss Mary Crofts and died as
headmaster of Skipton Grammar School, 22nd May, 1841.
Henry was sent to Rugby in September, 1852, after some
time at a preparatory school. His mother took a house
there in 1853. Sidgwick says that though ' successful in
schoolwork ' he had not been ' altogether happy ' at the
house where he had previously boarded, and he remained
' inobservant and bookish '.   He was not of the Tom Brown
type.   The chief influence [1] upon him at this time was that
of his second cousin, E. W. Benson, who afterwards married
his sister and died as Archbishop of Canterbury.   Benson
became a master in the school in 1852 and had already
helped Sidgwick in the study of Sophocles.   Though not his
tutor, Benson did much to stimulate Sidgwick's perception
of the charm of classical literature, and by certain religious
utterances ' startled ' him into a reverential appreciation
of the ' providential scheme of human history, which was
not soon to be forgotten '.   Sidgwick went to Trinity
College, Cambridge, instead of standing in accordance with
Rugby tradition for the Balliol Scholarship, because he knew
Benson's affection for Trinity.   His one ideal was to be a
scholar as like his cousin as possible.   For the present,
Sidgwick was a thoughtful schoolboy of unusual precocity
and the highest promise as a scholar.   In 1855 he left
Rugby as senior exhibitioner.

At Cambridge Sidgwick was probably the youngest man
of his year.   His career was a series of triumphs.   He won
a Bell Scholarship in 1856 ; the Craven Scholarship in 1857 ;
the Greek Epigram in 1858; and graduated in 1859 as thirty-
third wrangler and senior classic, winning also the first Chancellor's Medal.   He was elected to a Trinity Scholarship in
1857, and in 1859 became fellow and assistant tutor of his
college.   The normal sequel to such achievements would
have been a rise to the highest academical or ecclesiastical
positions.   He had, however, been led to a pursuit which
promised no such tangible rewards.   His autobiographical
fragment was written to explain how a central aim had
determined the course of his intellectual life even when it

---

[1] See Sidgwick's interesting reminiscences in the *Life of Benson*, vol.
i., pp. 145-151 and 249-255.

seemed 'most erratic and fitful'. He fortunately wrote enough to explain how this aim was suggested to him and affected his first philosophical studies. In the first volume of this journal Sidgwick gave an account of the position of such studies at Cambridge. The indifference of an earlier generation had been finally broken up by the influence of Whewell. Whewell had lectured upon Moral Philosophy ; he had introduced a paper upon philosophy into the fellow-ship examinations at Trinity, and he had procured the foundation of the Moral Sciences Tripos in 1851. A series of eminent lecturers at Trinity, Julius Hare, Thirlwall and Thompson, the last of whom had become Greek professor in 1853, had encouraged the study of Plato and Aristotle. The new tripos, however, had flagged, and was only ad-mitted as a qualification for a degree in 1860. Sidgwick, absorbed in his studies for the old triposes, did not become a candidate ; and he received no impulse from the official system. Cambridge, however, was to gain a philosopher by a kind of accident. In the beginning of his second year Sidgwick was invited to become an 'Apostle'. The invita-tion implied a high compliment from his ablest contem-poraries. He fortunately accepted it after some hesitation in admitting a distraction from his regular studies. The effect was remarkable. The society has from the days of Tennyson and Maurice included a remarkable number of very eminent men. They preserved the tradition of the famous 'band of youthful friends' described in "In Memoriam". To discuss all topics with perfect frankness and with 'any amount of humorous sarcasm and playful banter' was the practice ; and absolute candour the only duty enforced by the society. Any principle might be questioned, if questioned in sincerity; and Sidgwick observes characteristically that the apostles learnt to understand 'how much suggestion and instruction might be derived from what is in form a jest—even in dealing with the gravest matters'. 'The tie of attachment to the society formed,' he says, 'the strongest corporate bond which I have known in life.' It revealed to him that 'the deepest bent of his nature was towards' the life of thought—thought exercised 'upon the central pro-blems of human life'. He could not, however, for many years take the study of philosophy for his principal task. He was a poor man and his first duty was to support himself. He accepted, therefore, a classical lectureship in October, 1859, and for the first two years after his degree allowed himself to be 'seduced into private tuition'. He read philosophy during his vacations and was especially

interested by J. S. Mill, then at the height of his remarkable influence. He had also looked at Comte ' through Mill's
spectacles '.[1] He had not broken with the orthodox doctrine
in which he had been educated, but had become sceptical as
to many of its conclusions and especially as to the methods
of proof. He and his friends were convinced of the need of
a social reconstruction guided by scientific methods and of a
religious reform founded upon an examination of the evidence
for historical Christianity conducted ' with strict scientific
impartiality '. His striking remarks upon Tennyson's " In
Memoriam " explain his feeling.[2] He could never read the
lines beginning ' If e'er when faith had fallen asleep ' (in the
124th poem) without tears. " In Memoriam " had impressed
upon him ' the ineffaceable and ineradicable conviction that
humanity will not and cannot acquiesce in a godless world '.
He could not find rest in agnosticism, and, though accepting
the methods of modern science, revolted against its atheistic
tendencies. Mill's philosophy offered no solution of the great
difficulties. He oscillated for a time between religious and
philosophical studies, while, ' as a matter of duty,' he also
gave much thought to economic and social problems. In
1862 Renan's *Études d'histoire religieuse* suggested a new
line of inquiry. Wearied with the indecisive results of the
controversy between theologians and agnostics, he turned
to the investigation of religious history. In the autumn of
1862 he spent five weeks at Dresden, devoting his whole
time to the study of Arabic under a private tutor.[3] For the
next three years his spare time was given to Arabic and
Hebrew. He thought of aspiring to one of the two Arabic
professorships at Cambridge. They had the advantage of
being tenable by laymen, whereas the Knightbridge Professorship, which then expressly included Moral Theology,
would probably be given to a clergyman. He gradually
found that his Arabic studies would deduct too much time
from the study of the fundamental problems. The com-
parative history of Semitic religions which he had planned,
would, after all, not supply an answer to the great questions,
whether the doctrine of the Incarnation could be accepted as
historically true and what element of truth could be disengaged

---

[1] *Life of Benson*, ii., p. 249. Dr. Venn also tells me that for a time
Sidgwick seemed to be much attracted by positivism.

[2] *Tennyson's Life*, i., pp. 300-304.

[3] His friends speak of his having studied at Gottingen under Ewald,
and of his ambition to become the ' English Ewald '. I follow Sidgwick's
own account in his autobiographical fragment.

from the traditional creed. He turned again towards philosophy and worked hard to qualify himself as an examiner for the Moral Sciences Tripos in 1865 and 1866.

Dr. Venn informs me of another connexion which had some influence at this time. Venn had returned to Cambridge to lecture upon moral science; the only other lecturer in the same department was the Rev. J. B. Mayor of St. John's College, to whose influence upon Cambridge studies Sidgwick (in his article upon Cambridge philosophy) ascribes great weight. Venn, Mayor and Sidgwick, with a few later recruits, formed a society which was known to their friends as the Grote Club. They dined with John Grote, then Knightbridge professor, once a term at his vicarage at Trumpington, and afterwards read and discussed papers. Grote was a most efficient moderator, supplying a keen criticism and enforcing steady abstinence from digression. A certain affinity to his young friend is suggested by Sidgwick's remark that Grote's 'subtle and balanced criticism, varied and versatile sympathy, hardly qualified him—original as he was—to be founder of a school' Croom Robertson notes [1] that Grote invented certain phrases, 'felicific' and 'hedonics,' of which Sidgwick afterwards made use. In any case, Sidgwick's philosophical studies must have been encouraged and his dialectical acuteness sharpened in his debates with these congenial friends. In later years, Sidgwick belonged to other societies of a similar kind, especially to the Metaphysical Society, in which he crossed swords with Huxley, Mivart, W. G. Ward, Dr. Martineau, and other champions of various causes; to the 'Eranus,' a Cambridge body on the same model, and to the later Synthetical Society. They gave a most appropriate arena for the display of his characteristic powers. His early associates of the 'Apostolic' circle were struck by the 'amazing maturity' of his intellect. Though one of the youngest, he was already among the most competent. He had thought out the problems sufficiently to see the bearing of the various arguments, and would select some apparently trifling point assumed by his opponent and by a Socratic method bring out unexpected consequences with which it was pregnant. Socrates became a bore by pressing similar discussions upon unwilling ears. But Sidgwick's friends had invited the discussion, and, if a momentary vexation might follow a fair fall in the wrestling, his entire freedom from arrogance or dogmatism left no excuse for irritation. If he could not produce agreement he always

[1] In his life of Grote in the *Dictionary of National Biography*.

promoted good-will. If, as has been said, the Metaphysical
Society, died 'of love,' Sidgwick was one of the unintentional
assassins. His readiness to argue implied, not the pugnacity
which resents contradiction, but the desire to profit by it;
and the sense of humour shown in his 'Apostolic' banter
always played round his arguments. The foundation of
another society about 1862 illustrates one of the qualities
which added an extrinsic charm to his dialectical displays.
His elder brother, Mr. William Sidgwick, was at this time
a resident fellow at Oxford. The brothers founded the 'Ad
Eundem' Society, which met alternately at Oxford and
Cambridge for purely social purposes. Philosophising, if
not forbidden, was certainly not compulsory. The society
flourished, and Sidgwick attended a meeting within three
months of his death. I had the honour of being an early
member and, without offence to my comrades, I may safely
say that the expectation of meeting Sidgwick was always
one of the main inducements to attend; and that a pleasant
bond which kept up old college associations and enabled
representatives of the two universities to forgather on most
agreeable terms owed much of its strength to the Sidgwick
element. The charm of Sidgwick's society could be felt
even by those who cared nothing for philosophy.

The 'Ad Eundem' illustrated another point. It included
at starting such men as W. H. Thompson and W. G. Clark,
then public orator, who had long been the ornaments of the
upper sphere of academical society. Sidgwick, young as he
was, was already admitted to the friendship of his most
august seniors. In the following years, he gained the respect
of the upper academical circles, especially of the more intel-
lectually disposed, and his influence became potent among the
younger dons. The first great changes in the university system had taken place during Sidgwick's undergraduate career.
The proposal to abolish religious tests had afterwards come
to the front: and to carry a bill for that purpose through
Parliament was understood to be a necessary preliminary to
further reforms. Sidgwick took an important, though necessarily a subordinate, part in the agitation. In Trinity he was
one of a body of fellows led by J. L. Hammond, a man of
singular charm who was prevented by ill health from making
a mark proportioned to his great powers. In December,
1867, Sidgwick supported (and probably proposed) a resolution for abolishing the declaration imposed by the college
statutes. It was rejected; but Sidgwick's later action had
an indirect effect in securing the adoption of the policy. In
June, 1869, he accepted a lectureship in Moral Philosophy

in exchange for the classical lectureship, and now made up
his mind to attempt to found a philosophical school in
Cambridge. Meanwhile, he was pressed by the question
whether he had a moral right to retain his fellowship. The
problem involved some delicate casuistry. He had qualified
himself for the fellowship by a sincere declaration of belief.
Could he hold it, now that he could no longer make the
declaration? It might be urged that the legal measured the
moral obligation and that, as no one had a right to inquire
into his belief, he had a right to the position without regard
to his present beliefs. He tried, he says, to settle the point
'on general principles'. But Sidgwick was pretty sure to be
biassed by his own clear interests—that is, in the direction
opposed to them. Anyhow, he resigned his fellowship in
October, 1869. Sir George Young, a most competent wit-
ness, says in the *Cambridge Review* that the effect of his
resignation was very great. Fellows of other colleges followed
his example. An important meeting, held at Cambridge
in December, showed that a majority of residents was in
favour of the abolition; and a similar meeting at Oxford
two days before had been suggested by a knowledge of the
intended meeting at Cambridge. The parliamentary action
followed which led to the final abolition of tests in June, 1871.
How far Sidgwick's action had all the influence ascribed to
it can hardly be decided. Sidgwick would have been the
first to condemn any exaggeration of his own part. I must
therefore note that the parliamentary proceedings had shown
clearly that the main obstacle to a liberal success was the
abnormal slowness of the process of converting Gladstone
upon such questions, and that a more popular argument was
the disqualification for fellowships of the senior wranglers of
1860, '61 and '69. But there can be no doubt of the great
moral significance of Sidgwick's action. He was giving
up for a scruple, which to most people seemed refined, his
chief support and as it seemed the chances of academical
position. Happily by that time, the fellows of Trinity were
singularly free from any theological bigotry. Sidgwick was
permitted to retain his position as lecturer with the social
privileges of a fellow.

Sidgwick now began the course of teaching which continued through his life. In October, 1875, he became
Prælector on Moral and Political Philosophy in Trinity; and
in 1883 was elected to the Knightbridge Professorship upon
the death of Prof. Birks. He had been a candidate for the
post in 1872, when Birks succeeded F. D. Maurice. He
had not then published his great book. In 1883 his fitness

was so obvious that the election might be almost said to be by acclamation.

Sidgwick's influence as a lecturer was both important and characteristic in kind. The position of the study at Cambridge was so far unfavourable that his classes were necessarily very small. Sidgwick himself expressed some doubt as to the utility of metaphysical studies for men at the early age of his hearers. A youth, not endowed with a special predisposition, is more apt, he might think, to learn a philosophical jargon than to gain a clear insight into the real issues. This view prevented him at a later period, according to some of his colleagues, from pressing the claims of his own faculty so vigorously as they thought desirable. His own example, however, proves sufficiently that an aptitude for such study may show itself early and be well worth cultivation. I lately heard an intelligent person inquire what was the meaning of 'ethics'. Some explanation being offered, the inquiry arose how it could be possible to devote volumes to setting forth the objections to breaking the ten commandments. For practical purposes, perhaps, the state of that person was the more gracious; but Sidgwick's *Methods of Ethics*, of which his lectures were now giving the substance, would have answered the question effectually. To the select few his speculations revealed whole fields of interesting speculation. Sidgwick, of course, could hardly found a school in the ordinary sense. A 'Sidgwickian,' as connoting acceptance of a definite philosophical platform, would be almost a contradiction in terms. At anyrate where there were two Sidgwickians, they would necessarily resolve themselves into a debating society. Sidgwick had not the attraction of the teacher who has attained definite results and can give the watchword to a band of enthusiasts. His influence was free from the defects, if it had not the characteristic merits of such a position. It did not lead to ignoring difficulties but to facing them fairly. Though not claiming to have solved the great problems, he was fully convinced both that they were soluble, and that a man might well devote his life to hastening the solution. His subtlety in seeing difficulties and his candour in admitting them did not lead to a mere play of skilful dialectics. He set his hearers' minds to work and to work in the interest of truth. Several of his hearers have turned his lessons to good account; and have acknowledged most emphatically the debt which they owe to him. Close contact with such a man was no small part of 'a liberal education'. For Sidgwick had the ethical genius; and was as sensitive to the moral as some men to the æsthetic aspects of life. His transparent simplicity, extraordinary alertness of mind and intense love of truth enabled him to preach by the effectual method of personal contagion.

Meanwhile he had already taken up a function which absorbed much of his energy and fully illustrates his moral enthusiasm. Devotion to philosophy would not, he ·held, justify abstinence from the active duties of life. He desired to do something for the good of mankind and was naturally led to promote the education of women.[1] Girls had been admitted to the Cambridge examinations ; and in the autumn of 1869 Sidgwick thought out and proposed a scheme for providing lectures for the candidates. It was warmly taken up, and its success suggested the advantage of providing a house for the students in Cambridge. Sidgwick made himself responsible for the rent of such a house and in 1871 invited Miss Clough to undertake the superintendence. This again led to the formation of a company in 1874, to which Sidgwick subscribed money as well as labour ; and to the opening of Newnham Hall, built by the company in 1876. In that year Sidgwick married Miss Balfour. It would be as impertinent as happily it would be superfluous for me to speak of that event in any other way ; but its bearing upon this part of his career is matter of public knowledge. When in 1880 the North Hall was added to Newnham, Mrs. Sidgwick became vice-president, and the Sidgwicks took up their residence there till her resignation two years later. Sidgwick was a main supporter of the important measure by which, in 1881, women were admitted to the honours examination, and a great stimulus given to the movement. Upon Miss Clough's death, in 1892, Mrs. Sidgwick succeeded to her post, and the Sidgwicks resided in the college during the remainder of his life. Throughout the whole of this period Sidgwick, who had been the chief founder of the organisation, was at the heart of the resulting movement : suggesting the schemes which ultimately succeeded, advising Miss Clough through all her difficulties, taking the keenest interest in all the details of management, winning the affection of teachers and students by his social charm and judicious counsels, contributing munificently in money and taking the lead in the university legislation which was required by the novel experiment. He was always a member of the Council of Newnham, and was also for some years connected with the college at Girton. The main difference between the two

---

[1] I refer to the life of Miss Clough for full details.

bodies was that Sidgwick and the supporters of Newnham
were less anxious than their friendly rivals to assimilate the
education of women precisely to the system established for
men. For Sidgwick may be claimed, without hesitation, a
leading part in the remarkable changes which have trans-
formed the whole theory and practice of the higher education
of women in England.

Another set of duties fell to him in later years. The
University Commission of 1877 had been appointed in consequence of proposals by Cambridge Liberals which Sidgwick
helped to formulate. Not being a member of the govern-
ing body, he had no direct share in the changes made at
Trinity College under the Commission. The new statutes
for the university came into force in 1882. Sidgwick's value
was by this time fully appreciated in the university; and in
November, 1882, he became a member of the General Board
of Studies created under the new system. He held this
position till the end of 1899 and acted for several years as
secretary. He was also a member of the Council of the
Senate from 1890 to 1898. His colleagues on both speak
emphatically of his . conscientious discharge of his duties ;
his skill in debate and his power of incisive criticism tem-
pered by unfailing courtesy. The Cambridge system went
through very important changes, in which he played his
part. I am not qualified, nor would it be here possible, to
deal with questions of university politics ; but one or two
points, which I learn from Dr. Jackson, are characteristic.
The new order of things raised some delicate questions.
The taxation of the colleges for university purposes was
made burdensome by agricultural depression. Sidgwick, with
two colleagues, was appointed by the General Board to investigate the necessary rearrangement. He took the whole
work upon himself : collected all the information and devised
an elaborate scheme for settling the difficulty. He threw
himself heartily into financial problems and Dr. Jackson
thinks that he would have liked nothing better than to be
Chancellor of the Exchequer. He would have ' devised an
amazingly ingenious budget and his exposition would have
been a marvel of lucidity and address '. His scheme failed of
acceptance by an appearance of over subtlety, and Dr. Peile
admits that, if ever a doctrinaire, he was so on the General
Board. He delighted in framing schemes for compromise, and
became at times too obstinate in adhering to his own compromise. He had allowed so carefully for all interests that
any other arrangement seemed to him unjust. He was, it is
also suggested, so much interested in the details as occasion-

ally to lose sight of the broader and more obvious issues. No one, however, doubted the great value of his energetic co-operation in a period of important changes. When he indicated by giving up his place on the General Board that he was probably abandoning administrative work, says Dr. Jackson, the news seemed ' almost tragic '. It was ' like the parting of a parent and child '. One most tangible proof may be given of Sidgwick's keen interest in the reforms. The university was enabled by his munificence to introduce, or to hasten the introduction, of various additions to its agencies. He supplied the funds by which Dr. Maitland, now Professor, was restored to the university as reader in law; he helped in the same way to start the professorship now held by Dr. Ward, and he enabled the university to build a museum required by the School of Natural Sciences.

Sidgwick's final retirement from the Council was partly connected with the last phase of the question of admitting women to degrees. He never wished to adopt the university system of education for women without modification, and objected in particular to ' compulsory Greek '. He supported the proposal to grant titular degrees to women, though he had at first thought it premature or imprudent. Opponents thought that it was a step which would necessarily lead to further changes; Sidgwick and his friends considered it as a compromise for an indefinite time, though they could not pledge themselves to its absolute finality. The rejection by a great majority was a blow to the party of advance. Nobody could ever suspect Sidgwick of the slightest insincerity; but the measure advocated might seem equivocal, however good the motive : and a love of compromise, though prompted by simple desire for justice, may have an appearance of diplomacy.

Sidgwick's influence was for the moment injured; but he had other motives for not again standing for election to the Council. He was anxious to finish literary work, of which it is only strange that he had performed so much under so many distractions. Besides the duties already noticed he had from a very early time (certainly from 1864) taken an interest in ' Psychical Research '. The interest was connected with his course of speculation. His ethical position led him to desire some ' direct proof of continued individual existence '. He was president of the society founded in 1882 from 1882-1885, and again, 1888-1893 ; and for some time edited or superintended the editing of its journal. He brought to it all the conscientious spirit of scientific investigation ; and a desire to discover the truth of

alleged facts led him to investigate them with the most rigid
impartiality.   He was not the man to accept Don Quixote's
method of testing his armour leniently when he wished it to
be trustworthy.   He fully recognised and helped to expose
the impostures which obscured any real substratum of
truth.   Yet another application of his energy is mentioned
in the organ of the Charity Organisation Society.   He was
one of the founders of the Cambridge branch in 1879, having
previously belonged to the Mendicity Society.   He drew up
its rules, presided over the weekly meetings for many years,
contributed liberally, and was president till his death.   'It
will never be fully known,' it is added, 'how much of all
that is best in Cambridge to-day was due to his inspiration
and example.'

Sidgwick had found time in the midst of these labours to
produce his three books, the *Methods of Ethics* in 1874; the
Principles of Political Economy in 1883; and the *Elements of
Politics* in 1891.   He has also left work still in manuscript,
a considerable part of which will, it is hoped, be published.
The amount and quality of the purely intellectual work is
the more remarkable considering his activity in practical
directions.   I have tried, however, to indicate in how many
ways Sidgwick's employments fitted in with his pursuit of
philosophical truth.   A moralist is none the worse for some
practical acquaintance with applied morality.   His other
work gave weight to his convictions if it limited his output
within a moderate compass.   Indeed, considering the tempta-
tions of so versatile an intellect to excessive discursiveness,
his other occupations may well have suppressed only corollaries which though interesting would be, in strictness,
superfluous.

Sidgwick had hoped that after reaching sixty he might
resign his professorship to some worthy successor and devote
himself to finishing his literary work.   The warning that he
was suffering from a dangerous disease came to him early in
1900, and was accepted with the most admirable courage
and simplicity.   He afterwards read a paper at the Synthetic
Society and took part in the debate with his usual brilliancy.
Friends who met him still later, without being aware of his
position, found the old charm in his conversation and were
only impressed by a rather more marked tone of friendly
interest.   He resigned his professorship; quietly wound up
his affairs; and parted from life as nobly as he had lived it.
He died on 28th August, 1900.

A word or two upon personal characteristics may be permitted.   Sidgwick had no great physical power.   He suffered

a good deal from hay fever, and in late years from insomnia. He soothed hours of wakefulness by reading a great quantity of novels, and remembered their plots with singular retentiveness. Dr. Peile records that when meditating he liked to take a sharp walk, often 'breaking into a little run '. The starts indicated, perhaps, the flashing of some new thought upon his mind. The vivacity of such impressions made him one of the best of talkers. The difficulty of describing conversation is proverbial, and when I seek for appropriate epithets I am discouraged by the vagueness which makes them equally applicable to others. Henry Smith, for example, who often met Sidgwick at the 'Ad Eundem,' had an equal fame for good sayings; and both might be credited with unfailing urbanity, humour, quickness and other such qualities. Their styles were nevertheless entirely different, while to point out the exact nature of the difference is beyond my powers. Smith, perhaps, excelled especially in the art of concealing a keen epigram in a voice and manner of almost excessive gentleness. Sidgwick rather startled one by sudden and unexpected combinations and arch inversions of commonplace. His skill in using his stammer was often noticed. His hearers watched and waited for the coming thought which then exploded the more effectually. Sidgwick not only conceded but eagerly promoted contributions of talk from his companions. He would wait with slightly parted lips for an answer to some inquiry, showing a keen interest which encouraged your expectation that you were about to say a good thing, and sometimes, let us hope, helped to realise the expectation. He differed from Smith—who preserved a strict reticence upon the final problems—by a readiness to discuss any question whatever, if it were welcome to his companions. He was not only perfectly frank but glad to gain enlightenment even from comparatively commonplace minds. Johnson commended a talker who would fairly put his mind to yours. That marks one of Sidgwick's merits. He would take up any topic; made no pretension to superiority, and was as willing to admit ignorance or error as he was always fertile in new lights. He delighted in purely literary· talk; and his criticisms happily combined two often inconsistent qualities: the freshness of impression which suggests a first reading of some book, with the ripeness of judgment which implies familiarity with the book and its writer. He might, I think, have been the first of contemporary critics had he not devoted his powers to better things. Sidgwick could not be unconscious of his own abilities; but was as free from arrogance as from any approach to ostentation; and, in

fact, freedom from the weaknesses of morbid self-conscious-
ness was one of his most obvious characteristics. When he
resigned his fellowship, he made no fuss about doing a simple
act of duty; and when the fatal sentence was pronounced,
he accepted it with perfect quietness, without complaint,
and with no display of resignation. There was no merit in
Boswell's good humour, said Burke, it was so natural. I
had the same feeling about Sidgwick's unselfishness and high
principle. I fancied that he could not really have a conscience
—much as he professed to esteem that faculty—because I
could not see that his conscience could ever have anything
to do. He had plenty of scruples, because he saw the full
complexity of any special case; but, when he had the facts
properly arranged, the decision to act followed spontaneously.

I must try to indicate in a few words the relation between
Sidgwick's thought and his personal characteristics. I may
take for granted the singular activity and subtlety of his
intellect. The whole substance of his books is logic, with
a minimum of amplification or rhetoric. They are a con-
tinuous and unflagging scrutiny of the positions to be established or confuted. The subtlety again is always at the
service of common sense. It is directed to secure clearness
and solidity, not the construction of an elaborate system.
I remember his once speaking of certain philosophies. They
resemble cardhouses : you can perhaps coax your first principle into an appearance of stable equilibrium; but when
you build a second upon the first and go on to a third and
fourth, the collapse of the whole edifice is certain. It was
therefore Sidgwick's aim to lay secure foundations on solid
ground. He has given in a fragment (to be published in a
forthcoming edition) a 'genetic account' of his book upon
ethics. He had been repelled by Whewell's arbitrary system
of intuitions, and attracted by the plain common sense of
Mill's Utilitarianism. But difficulties revealed themselves
which sent him to all the great moralists from Aristotle to
Butler and Kant. The final result seemed to some of his
critics to be a rehabilitation of Utilitarianism. He protested
against this view and said that he had criticised Utilitarianism as unsparingly as Intuitionism. He had 'transcended'
the difference; or (as he says in the fragment) become a
Utilitarian on an Intuitionist basis. The first principle of
Utilitarianism is 'the most certain and comprehensive of
Intuitions'. But the reconciliation itself brings out most
sharply a fundamental contrast—that, namely, between this
first principle and the conflicting principle of 'rational

egoism '. It is ' reasonable ' to seek our own happiness ; and yet it cannot be proved empirically that this harmonises with the other reasonable principle of seeking the general happiness. Conduct, then, cannot be made ' intrinsically reasonable ' without accepting a hypothesis ' unverifiable by experience '. Unless, therefore, we can believe that the moral order imperfectly realised in this world is actually perfect, the ' cosmos of duty is really reduced to a chaos ' and the attempt to form a perfect ideal of rational conduct fore-doomed to inevitable failure. Sidgwick, that is, had not found a final solution for the old Utilitarian difficulty. A sufficient criterion of morality could be found in the 'greatest happiness ' principle ; but the difficulty was to discover a sufficient ' sanction '. How much this difficulty affected Sidgwick is shown by his remarks upon " In Memoriam ". He frankly admitted that he could not give a solution. Meanwhile, whatever the true answer, the effect of his elaborate scrutiny into the fundamental conceptions of Ethics gave, as I think from my own experience and that of others, the most important of all modern contributions towards a clear realisation of the conditions of approaching the problems involved.

A similar tendency marks his *Political Economy.* His early interest in social problems had led him to the subject. His love of all intellectual activities took him far into some tech-nical discussions, upon bimetallism for example, which have little bearing upon ethics. But his main point is closely connected with the problem of what Bentham called 'self-regarding conduct '. He had been again greatly influenced by Mill. He adopts old methods, but endeavours to restate the results so as to meet later criticisms. The ' classical economists ' had insisted upon the supreme importance of self-interest and had deduced the *laissez faire* doctrine. Sidgwick by a careful and acute investigation of their arguments tries to recognise the true place of the 'self-interest ' principle, and to get rid of the excessive abso-lutism of his predecessors. He refutes in particular, the ' wage fund ' theory, which had been used as an argument against the possibility of social improvement. The old rigid system is thus broken down, and free play is left for hopes of social regeneration. It is, however, equally characteristic that Sidgwick endeavours to do full justice to the importance of the self-interest principle, which had been unduly magnified into the sole axiom of political economy; and, without adopting the old *non possumus,* emphasises the necessity of appealing to experience. He is characteristically opposed [1] to the claims of sociologists, who have jumped prematurely to general theories of society which would invalidate or absorb political economy; and to such followers of the historical school as incline to deny the possibility of anything beyond purely empirical results. Sidgwick's mixture of cautious scrutiny with a hearty respect for the common sense embodied in the old system is again conspicuous.

Both in the *Ethics* and the *Political Economy*, his common sense leads him to assign less importance than many of his contemporaries to evolutionist theories. They tend, he clearly holds, to exaggerated claims of scientific infallibility and after all leave the fundamental questions to be answered. If you could show how morality has come into being, you would not show what it actually is. The effect of his position is marked in the *Elements of Politics*. He was always keenly interested in political questions and showed his characteristic common sense in speaking of them. There is abundance of that quality in the *Politics*, when he again expressly takes up the line of Bentham and his followers. We have the old problem of the proper relation between the State and the Individual, or self-interest and public spirit. Common sense is invaluable; but I confess that to my mind it is impossible to discuss political questions effectively without constant reference to historical development; and that, from the absence of such reference, Sidgwick's book is rather a collection of judicious remarks than a decided help to the formation of political theory. He afterwards, I believe from a sense of this weakness in his method, took up some historical investigations into political institutions and delivered lectures upon the topic. I do not know whether they were sufficiently finished to justify republication, or how they might be related to the general treatise.

Sidgwick published nothing, I think, expressly treating of the ultimate problems which always occupied his mind. Friends have told me that in later life he drew rather nearer to orthodox views. The Synthetic Society, of which he was an important member, endeavours, I understand, to promote efforts towards a reconstructive process with which he no doubt strongly sympathised. He perhaps felt that he had no definite help to give to the solution of the final difficulty suggested in the conclusion of the *Ethics*, or hoped that he might be able to utter his convictions more fully when he

---

[1] See his "Scope and Method of Economic Science" (address to the British Association, 1885).

was relieved from the pressure of his active employments; and could complete his speculative labours, if not by offering a full answer to his doubts, yet by indicating the best method of approximating to such a result.

A meeting of Sidgwick's friends was held at Cambridge upon the 26th November. It was resolved to raise funds for some memorial; but it is not yet decided whether it should be a library of philosophical books, a studentship in philosophy or a lectureship in moral science.

THE ABERDEEN UNIVERSITY PRESS LIMITED.

www.ingramcontent.com/pod-product-compliance
Ingram Content Group UK Ltd.
Pitfield, Milton Keynes, MK11 3LW, UK
UKHW042151280225
455719UK00001B/277